by Edward Sanders

Poem from Jail (1963)

Peace Eye (1966)

The Family: The Manson Group and Aftermath (1971, New Edition, 1990)

Egyptian Hieroglyphics (1973)

Tales of Beatnik Glory, Volume 1 (1975)

Investigative Poetry (1976)

20,000 A.D. (1976)

Fame & Love in New York (1980)

The Z-D Generation (1981)

The Cutting Prow (1983)

Hymn to Maple Syrup & Other Poems (1985)

Thirsting for Peace in a Raging Century: Selected Poems 1961–1985 (1987)

Poems for Robin (1987)

Tales of Beatnik Glory, Volumes 1 & 2 (1990)

Hymn to the Rebel Cafe (1993)

Chekhov (1995)

1968: A History in Verse (1997)

EDWARD SANDERS

1968

A HISTORY IN VERSE

BLACK SPARROW PRESS
SANTA ROSA ■ 1997

1968: A HISTORY IN VERSE. Copyright © 1997 by Edward Sanders.

ACKNOWLEDGMENTS

Thanks to Miriam for her vast memory and her drawing of the Pulse Lyre, to Tuli Kupferberg and M.L. Liebler for the loan of some books, to John Sinclair for filling me in on hashhoney Sunday, to Sam Leff for the tape from Lincoln Park, to Bob Fass for items from his archives, and to Austin Metz for scanning the images.

Black Sparrow Press books are printed on acid-free paper.

LIBRARY OF CONGRESS CATALOGING-IN-PUBLICATION DATA

Sanders, Ed.
    1968 : a history in verse / Edward Sanders.
        p.   cm.
    ISBN 1-57423-037-9 (paper : alk. paper). — ISBN 1-57423-038-7 (cloth trade : alk. paper). — ISBN 1-57423-039-5 (signed cloth : alk. paper)
        1. Nineteen sixty-eight, A.D.—Poetry. 2. United States—History—1961–1969—Poetry. I. Title.
PS3569.A49A616 1997
811'.54—dc21   97-18698
                                                                                CIP

From the Author

I will not pretend
that I was a very big part
        of '68

I surged through the year   on my own little missions
most of them not much matter now

but then I strutted through the time-track
daring to be part
      of the history
         of the era

& believing that huge change was imminent—
that the United States
          would become more free and sharing
that poverty would be banished
and racism ebb
    very very quickly
        by the time we were middle aged.

Many names & illustrious events no doubt
      I have neglected, passed over, or subsumed
      in someone else's tale.

For that I apologize,
but this is the '68
      whose pulses still surge
           in my psyche

1968

A HISTORY IN VERSE

This poem is dedicated
to the memory of
the great bard Allen Ginsberg

1968

Out of the Summer of Love
came an Exorcism Fall
& a chilly winter

On New Year's Eve
the Fugs sang their final set
at the Player's Theater
                on MacDougal Street
after two years of perfs
                and 600 shows
I rented my final limousine
        and pretended to be rich
going to parties in the Lower East Side

and then it was time for '68
                the year the people spoke
                                for the Iron Polis.

A beaknosed guy named James Earl Ray
went to a hypnotist in L.A.
                        on January 4
(He'd been seeing hypnos
 now and then

since coming to California
                the fall of '67

and sped up
his phone installation
by claiming he was working
to get George Wallace on the
                        presidential ballot)

Zoom! Shree! Ack! Crash!
Four U.S. planes down over 'Nam
        on January 5

with the total above 5,000

↗   ↗   ↗   ↗
grief grief grief grief
↘   ↘   ↘   ↘

but nothing I've read of January 5
adds up the napalm or agent orange
        (or the evil fragmentation bombs)

Also on January 5
   Benjamin Spock and four others
       were indicted for counseling young men
           to avoid the draft•

and on the 9th
       Sweden granted asylum to four U.S. Navy guys
          who had deserted in Japan

January 10th, a conference at the White House
          on Domestic Intelligence
chaired by Joseph Califano, special assistant to Johnson
Among those there:
Under Secretary of Defense Paul Nitze
Army General Counsel Robert Jordan, III
AG Ramsey Clark
Dep AG Warren Christopher

     They wanted better data on discord
     after the '67 summer riots,
     and the October March on the Pentagon•

There was a meeting
       on January 11th
at Anita and Abbie's on St. Marks
We were there to plan
     a visit to America
       by a party of dissidence

Rubin wanted to call it the
                Youth International Party
Krassner blurted out
        "We'll be Yippies!"

We shouted with excitement and laughter

Police then and now
      are often too fond of the pot bust
so there was a lot of outrage
      for a pre-dawn bu sweep
           on the 17th
by 200 cops
      at the SUNY Stony Brook campus,
      in Suffolk County, Long Island
The fuzz had floor plans and dorm keys
They tipped off reporters
and gave them a
      little booklet,
   "Operation Stony Brook"
      with maps and descriptions
        of the students they were looking to book

38 were cuffed and vanned

      Dawn raids
      at houses of learning
      are an insult
        to Hathor

the goddess of schools.

January 19
       James Earl Ray enrolled
       in a 6-week bartending course in L.A.

       Sharon Tate
              wed Roman Polanski
              in London
                     on January 20
       They were there for the
       premiere of *Rosemary's Baby*
       and soon to return to L.A.
              where they stayed for a while
                     in a fourth floor apartment
                           at the Chateau Marmont Hotel

The Fugs had a new record out called *Tenderness Junction*
with jacket photos by Richard Avedon
              One of its best tracks
              was the "Exorcism of the Pentagon"
              of 10-21-'67
              when we rented a flat bed truck
              and stood on it
                    in the Pentagon parking lot
              with San Francisco Diggers
              chanting "Out Demons Out!"

We'd signed with Warner/Reprise
                  after being tossed off Atlantic Records
                  and in January had begun to record our next•

We played the Psychedelic Supermarket
in Boston
       the same weekend
       Ms. Tate married Mr. Polanski
       (a place now long since gone—it's now,
       I'm told, a biomedical research
       facility for Boston University—
       and maybe it was then too)

A soldier named Ron Kovic was injured
the Saturday the Fugs sang "Kill for Peace" in Boston
                              by Vietnamese firing from a graveyard
He was taken to intensive-care in Danang
Given last rites, told he'd never walk
He glanced around the ward
at the legless
a child without arms
a baby burned by napalm
                    men with gaping brains
         a Green Beret who screamed
                         each night for his mother
a black pilot bloating into convulsions—
the sights & sounds & smells of wardeath's suturing anthems

At North Star Bay in Greenland
in the evening of Jan 21
         a B-52 with four atomic bombs
                    crashed near the U.S. base at Thule

Denmark was angry
that U.S. planes
         had flown above its lands
& reaffirmed its policy to forbid
                    atomic planes overhead

The American war caste smiled
                    in its rivers of nukes

Honk honk
go the geese of Canada

From January 22 to 27
    The Fugs were in Montreal
    at a club called the New Penelope
    I asked Jake Jacobs
                 to join us for the gigs
    He had a beautiful voice
    Few things are as thrilling

13

as singing with another person
whose voice helps weave
that mantra-seed cloth
so cherished by Erato and Calliope

The Fugs drove to farmland outside Montreal
in their psychedelic garb
rented snowmobiles

& then sped arabesquedly
through fresh fallen snow
howling & growling
in long curving arcs
& random ornateness,
peace signs &
the 8's of Forever
in the gas-eating thrill zones of Gone.

On the 25th
Bob Segren
vaulted 17′ 4¼″
at the Millrose Games
at MSG

On January 28 the Fugs
played a club called The Trauma in Philadelphia
always a good party town
The place was so packed with half clothed bodies
we could barely get on stage

We returned to the Lower East Side
in time for the
Tet Offensive
on January 30.

They planned it
from a huge tunnel complex
northwest of Saigon
with 150 miles of tunnels on three levels
humid and slithery
about two feet wide and two high

dug during the 30 years of liberation

There were underground rooms:
        hospitals for instance

        On the 31st
        the Viet Cong entered the presidential palace
        and the U.S. embassy in Saigon
                holding it six hours

        In Hue
        the U.S. used gas, and bombs,
            to try to dislodge the
                Viet Cong invaders
        for days
        till the Marines reclaimed the city.

Fortune Magazine
        in its January issue
            said that the most alarming aspect
                of the youth revolution
      was its hesitance to consume,
          a huge threat
              to the American Way

Quack quack
go the ducks of derision

      Also in January
      at the Army's Dugway Proving Grounds
sixty Miles southwest of Salt Lake City

    a deathwaft
        of nerve gas
          escaped
      and killed around 5,000 sheep
              on nearby farms

Honk honk
go the geese of Canada

On February 1
good people winced
at the image of terror
          shown 'round the world
Justice CIA-style
     as General Nguyen Loan
               shot a Viet Cong suspect in the head
                         in public, for the cameras.

Quack quack
go the ducks of derision

          I helped write a press release
          signed by Abbie Hoffman, Jerry Rubin, Paul Krassner
                                        and myself

          for the birth of Yippie
          and the Festival of Life

               Arlo Guthrie, Country Joe & the Fish
               The Fugs, and Allen Ginsberg
               were so far the biggest "draws"
     but the idea was to get the Beatles, the Rolling Stones and Dylan

                    It seemed such an excellent concept—
                    a Festival of Life!

                    in a city where L.B.J.
                    was coming for his crown
                              in a doomdome of death

                    so natural and Tom Paine-ish
                    to rouse up a 6-day Festival
                    where Be-In & Love-In
                                        turned left.

          The spirit of the Digger Free Store
                              would suffuse it
          —free food, free music, free pot and loitering love
          I liked it
          We planned a daily newspaper
          There'd be a night where
                    100,000 people would burn their draft cards

with the world "Beat Army"
                              written in flame

"We demand the Politics of Ecstasy!"
                    our leaflets thundered.
"Rise up and Abandon the Creeping Meatball!"
—though, 30 years later, it seems a tactical error
to announce that 500,000 people
               were going to make love
                         in Chicago parks

    for most Americans
          didn't want kids
               fucking in the streets.

The Fugs flew to California
        to play the Avalon Ballroom on Feb 3
                    at Sutter & Van Ness•

    At a psychedelic club
    you played with images projected across you

    It was good for the ego
               to dissolve in the visual gestalt

On Sunday, February 4
Neal Cassady went to a wedding in
                    San Miguel de Allende
He'd left his bag at a railroad station
               a few miles away
and after the party
          the legend goes
Neal went hopping
     down the tracks to get it back
          counting the ties
               stoned on tequila & seccies
                    one two three four...

when he tumbled down roll-eyed

17

the muse of novels
                a psychedelic bus
                            & a hundred good poems.

Jimi Hendrix finished his album
                        Axis: Bold as Love
and was touring the States—
On February 6
he flame-Strat'd in front of 20,000
                            at Arizona State
On February 8 he played
with Eric Burdon and the Animals in Anaheim

The Fugs performed with Burdon and the An's
a day or two later
                at the Santa Barbara fairgrounds

    We were leaving after the gig
    There were teen-shrieks in the lobby

            clumping feet
            and the sharp slide of fingernails
                            on post-perf skin

    It was the only time
    I ever had my clothes torn off
    —not quite the fun once imagined—
                with rip-sounds of button holes
                            and the faint clicks
    of buttons on concrete
                    racing to
                        rented cars.

    In San Francisco I went to see Hendrix backstage
                            at the Winterland
    where he was making movies
                        with an 8 mm cam
    I wanted to ask him
                to sing at the Festival of Life

    I remembered how one night on MacDougal Street

he'd told me he hated his singing voice
I told him, "Man, you have a beautiful voice"
or, in Egyptian,

a kherew   nefer
vox   *pulcherrima.*

During this trip
   I helped Michael McClure
   record some tunes at a studio in San Francisco

   Michael played autoharp
        and it was not easy keeping him close to
   the microphone
   in his agitated strumming
   laying down ditties such as
"The Allen Ginsberg for President Waltz"
   and "Oh Lord, Won't you Buy Me a Mercedes Benz"
        the latter made famous later
                by Janis Joplin

   We watched his play, *The Beard*
   with its famous cunnilingus scene
          'tween Jean Harlow and Billy the Kid

In Los Angeles we appeared on the Les Crane TV show
Phil Ochs was there
      in the audience
        and after that he was my friend
Then the Fugs flew up to Seattle for a concert
        and back to the Lower East Side.

      In early February
         while the Fugs were in Cal.
      there was a famous garbage strike in NYC
      Miriam was talking to her mother
      and looking out of our second story window
              at 196 Avenue A

(an old dental office with a marble fireplace
pricey at $150 a month)
she saw that the phone booth
across the street was
entirely covered with trash!!!

Down in Memphis
the garbage workers were
treated like dirt
There were 1,300 of them, mostly black
—low paying jobs, no job security, no insurance
They hauled the garbage around in old leaky leather tubs
on their shoulders
and no place for shelter in the rain
because white folk didn't want them on their porches.

The workers were members of
the American Federation of State
County and Municipal Employees
but the city refused to recognize them

Two workers
got into the barrel of their truck
a big cylinder with
a built-in compactor
during a rain storm

and were crushed

A few days after the crush
there was another rainy day

the mostly white supervisors were permitted to wait in the barns
playing cards till the rain stopped
and were paid for the full day

but 22 black workers were told to go out and collect it
in the rain
or not get paid

They went home

and were paid two hours.
So, on Lincoln's birthday, February 12
they struck

emboldened by the famous New York City strike
whose phone-engulfing
visuality
so startled Miriam
as she talked with her mother.

The Olympic Games at Grenoble
brought grace
to thirsty eyes

Jean-Claude Killy, three gold medals
for grace on skis
Eugenio Monti, age 40,
gold on 2-man and 4-man bobsleds

In ice hockey the Czechs beat the USSR by 5-4
though the USSR in weeks
would use their tanks as hockey pucks

Peggy Fleming grace-dazzled the ice
with a double axel 'tween what the Britannica called
"two smoothly controlled
spread eagles"

In another part of the world
a young man named Sirhan Bishara Sirhan
had been employed as a exercise boy
on a thoroughbred horse ranch
in Corona outside L.A.
and hungered to be a jockey
September '67 he fell from a horse,
and though his injuries were not serious—
he had blurred vision and pain,
and gave up his passion to race.

He lived with his mom in Pasadena
& dropped out of sight
                        'tween January and March '68

It may have been then
they made him into a patsy,
                        or a programed assassin. •

In *The Search for the "Manchurian Candidate,"* John Marks quoted
an unidentified CIA researcher, from the old days, who alleged it
would be much easier to make a "patsy" programmed to "make
authorities think the patsy committed a particular crime," than to
program a robot assassin. Hypnosis expert Milton Kline, unpaid
consultant to CIA researchers, guessed to Marks he could
                        fashion a patsy
                        in a mere three months.

    Sirhan was very, very easily hypnotized

February 15
    The National Security Council
    did away with draft deferments
                        for most grad students
                        and occupational deferments too

        February 19 Oscar Nominations:
        Ann Bancroft for *The Graduate*
        Faye Dunaway for *Bonnie and Clyde*
        Dustin Hoffman for *The Graduate*
                Spencer Tracy for *Guess Who's Coming to Dinner?*
        Paul Newman for *Cool Hand Luke*
                Rod Steiger for *In the Heat of the Night*
                Warren Beatty for *B & C.*

I'd been on a panel about The New Journalism at Dartmouth
on January 17 with Jack Newfield
I told him the Fugs and Allen Ginsberg were going to perform
                        in Appleton, Wisconsin
        where Senator McCarthy was buried

Jack suggested we exorcise his grave

Thus was born the
                 Exorcism of Senator Joseph McCarthy's
                 Gravesite

We flew to Appleton on Feb 19
and played the Cinderella Ballroom

                 Nothing much of interest
                 a place more usually devoted to
                 polka concerts
                         and chicken dinners
                 except that during the break
                 a deputy from the Winnebago County Sheriff's Dept
                 came up and said
                 "I don't care what you sing,
                 but if you jack off that microphone
                                         one more time
                 I'm going to arrest you."

The next morning we were driven to
                         the cemetery
I glanced at the headlines of that day's
                 Appleton Post-Crescent:
SAIGON AWAITING NEW ATTACK BY COMMUNISTS
& TREASON LAW INTRODUCED FOR HELPING HANOI

                 It was surreal and chilly
                 an excedrin morning
                         after a 5 AM party
                 our toothpaste-scurry breaths
                                 in chilly clouds
                 by Mr. McCarthy's
                         unimposing 'taph

                 Ginsberg and I conferred on
                         a proper flow for the rite
                 There were about 50 people there
                 mostly students from Lawrence U
                         the sponsor of our performance.

23

A limber-limbed damzel lay down by the grave
                                        to kiss the ghost
            and later sat across its granite top
                        beauteous in the clear winter morn—

I wonder what happened to her
            phantom of photos
                        now decades old

            Here's what we did:

1. Ginsberg stood in the face of the stone
    and chanted the Dharani spell
                        to remove disasters

    He'd brought his harmonium

2. He then created a circle
                by walking around the participants
                        intoning the Tibetan spell
                            to banish malevolent spirits:

                Om Raksha
                Raksha
                Om Om Om
                Phat Svaha
                        six times

3. We asked those present
                to place things of offering
                            on the gravestone

    Food and flowers were bestowed above
                and a few marijuana seeds were planted
                                    in the sod

4. Ginsberg recited the Hebrew prayer for food

5. Then the Mantram for the Invocation of Shiva: Purification
    of Bhang:
                Om Aing Ghring Cling Chamunda Yea Vijay!

6. Next was a sing-song
             chanting of deities and power-words
                        by Edward Sanders
   in the mode of what he'd done at the Pentagon Exorcism
   to conjure the ghost.

   Nothing overt occurred
              no hover-job, no mist, no noise, no clank, no rustle

7. Next was an invocation to bisexual Greek and
   Indian deities (since McCarthy was a notorious
   baiter of homosexuals)

8. We recited the Prajna Paramita Sutra
                  to purify the ghost of McCarthy
   with Sanders sitting in on the harmonium

9. The group sang "My Country 'Tis of Thee"

10. Ginsberg suggested we sing "Hare Krishna"
                 —so we did, six times through

11. Ken Weaver suggested, "Let's sing 'Hey, Joe'"
    Sanders: "Hey, Joe, where you gonna go?" (laughter)
    Weaver: "with that subpoena in your hand."

12. The purified and exorcised Spirit was then sent
                 back up to the sky
                         or to its, uh, appointed Karma realm
    by the Ceremony of the Greater Hexagram
             followed by the last words
             of Plato's Republic:
                 εὖ πράττωμεν
             "We shall fare well"

   It was over.
       Tuli Kupferberg said, "So long, Joe."
                 and we walked down the hill to our cars

I went back and jotted down what offerings lay
                          on the top of his stone:
There was a bottle of Midol, a ticket to the movie *The War Game*,
a Spring Mobilization Against the War leaflet, English leather stick

cologne, a stuffed parrot, one candy bar, chapstick, one dozen red
roses, one dozen white geraniums, one dozen yellow geraniums, one
"Get Fugged" button, some coins, sugar wafers, coat buttons
                         plus two seeds of marijuana.

        And then, as usual for a year of bullets
        we flew away,
                and left the locals to sort out
                        the knots of what we had done.•

                The next night we played in a large agricultural pavilion
                at the University of Wisconsin in Madison
                where there were huge pigs in pens
                                outside our dressing room
                that jostled and oinked
                                as we trotted onto the shrieky stage.

February 22
        the good part of Lyndon Johnson
                proposed to Congress to build 6 million low & mid income
        units in urban areas by 1978

In Stockholm
        the Minister of Education Olof Palme
spoke to 6,000 people holding candles
against the U.S. war

It looked for a while as if the U.S. would
sever diplomatic relations.

                                PIGASUS

        The Yippies decided to run a pig for president
        At first Rubin called it Bancroft P. Hogg
        but a much better name was found:
                                        Pigasus

        I went along with it
                hoping it would help stifle

26

                                    a certain use of the name

            for I could never join in on the rhythmic chants
            of the Panthers at demos:
                        "No more brothers in jay-all
                        Off th' pi-ig!
                        No more brothers in jay-all
                        Off th' pi-ig!..."

                  just as I thought it was a mistake
                  for the Futurists
                  to call the Austrian gendarmes
                                          "walking pissoirs."

      The first Yippie action
            was Feb 27, in response to the dawn pot raid
            at the State University at Stony Brook
                                          a month before
            We went to the gates of the school at dawn
            and sang through microphones—
                  The Fugs, Country Joe and the Fish,
                        the Pageant Players, and a group called
                                          Soft White Underbelly

It got what everybody wanted: publicity
There was a picture of me
                  in my long hairy-grey dress coat
and our guitarist Ken Pine
                        in the *Daily News*

while the *N.Y. Post* made note that
            "Timothy Leary predicts that 100,000 dancing, joyous
            yippies will swarm over Chicago's airports so the
            Presidential plane cannot land at convention
            time."

                  It was at the Stony Brook gig
                  tired at dawn
                  I began to feel the long, craving shame
                                    for some of my work
                  I didn't have the type

                                                            27

of idealistic and topical repertoire
                    to inspire the streets
& I didn't take the time to research & write them

Instead I was working on tunes like
"Johnny Pissoff Meets the Red Angel"
                    & "Ramses the II is Dead, My Love"
which we were about to record
to follow up *Tenderness Junction*

so we chugged through our repertoire
of "Nothing," "Kill for Peace," "Saran Wrap" et cetera
                    huffing out phonemes of winter steam
                    unable to look at the
                              sleepy crowd
                              just five feet away

In the afternoon after the dawn at Stony Brook
I signed a lease for a new location
                    of the Peace Eye Bookstore

THE PEACE EYE BOOKSTORE

I rented an old kosher meat market
in late '64
        at 383 East 10th, near Avenue C
I kept the words "STRICTLY KOSHER" in place
above the Hebrew letters

and added a sign adorned
                    with Eyes of Horus
It was there Tuli Kupferberg & I formed the Fugs
had our first rehearsals
It was there I published
              the final issues
                    of *Fuck You/ A Magazine of the Arts*

It was a famous little three room place
                    built like a railroad flat
LEMAR was founded there
We printed hundreds of leaflets

posters, booklets & poems
on the back room mimeo
and writers and singers from all over the world
found their way there
to sit on the red couch
in the front room.

The police raided in '66
and busted me for my magazine
The ACLU took the case
and finally,
after something like 17 court dates
a 3-judge panel
found me not guilty
during the Summer of Love of '67

For a while during Love Year
I'd given Peace Eye over to the "Community"
and the community
turned it for a few weeks into a crashpad

with mattresses in all three rooms
A charismatic youth named Groovy
took charge
until the landlord forced me to call it off
(I was still paying the rent)
and the place reverted back to a bookstore

A few weeks later Groovy and a woman
named Linda Fitzpatrick
               were murdered a block away
                              with furnace bricks
                       in a bare bulb mattress basement

It was a famous case they said foretold
                              the death of flowers

After that I left Peace Eye dormant
               caught in the pleasant pincers
                       of carousing, recording and fame
               till the spring of '68
       when I was determined
                       to bring it back to power

and so the afternoon
                       following the cold dawn concert at Stony Brook
I signed a lease to move Peace Eye to 147 Avenue A
between 9th and 10th opposite the park
a place that had housed
                       the *East Village Other*
I gave the *Other* $500 in key money
and hired people to get it ready—
scraping, painting, putting in shelves

The artist Spain Rodriguez
who'd painted the groovy sign
               for the Digger Free Store
                       around the corner

did the new Peace Eye sign
 —chrome yellow letters on red—
  and a fine Eye of Horus

On February 29
 Defense Secretary Robert MacNamara left office
  waving his arm up high in the
   front page *New York Times* photo
  but letting none know of his
   qualms about the war

CIA CHAOS

During these months
 the movement called the Resistance
  which had begun in April of '67
  when 75 burned their draft cards
  at the Sheep Meadow in Central Park
   grew mightily
    and attracted the stern attention
     of the CIA's Chaos program

  a six-year domestic program
 set in motion by CIA director Richard Helms
   to squash domestic dissent.

Operation Chaos grew out of an investigation of *Ramparts*
a left-liberal investigative magazine.
CIA learned in Jan '67 that *Ramparts* was going to do an exposé of
the fact that the National Student Association was funded by CIA.

Ramparts had run big ads on February 14, '67
in the *Washington Post & N.Y. Times*
announcing a big article in its March issue:

"The CIA has infiltrated and subverted the country's student
leadership. It has used students to spy. It has used students to
pressure international student organizations into Cold War
positions, and it has interfered in a most shocking manner in
the internal workings of the nation's oldest and largest student
organization."

The CIA went tweedily bonkers
Right away a rightist breakin man
had stolen the *Ramparts* CIA files
and they were brought to D.C.
where two CIA officers
took a look at them.

They created some detailed files on *Ramparts* backers
and sicced the IRS on as many as they could

Then, in August of '67, the CIA began its enormous
and mostly still-secret program called Operation Chaos•
for spying on and and
looking for ways to
stymie the anti-war left
The Underground Press was one of the Chaos program's targets
as we shall see later on in the
chrono-flow

THE CIA'S OPERATION RESISTANCE

Circa December 1967
A CIA Chaos sub-scheme called
Operation Resistance was set up,
ostensibly to dig up data to help "protect"

CIA recruiters on campuses•
It was an Operation Resistance officer
who later came up with the scheme
             to destroy the underground press,
                              as we shall see.

        The CIA in 1968 spent our tax money
        to index some 50,000 members of the
        California Peace and Freedom party
        One of hundreds of antiwar
                   groups
                   the CIA surveilled.

        Thank you, o twerps.

On March 2
        the human named James Earl Ray
                got his diploma
                        from the International Bartending School
        and on the 5th
                had the sharp tip of his nose
                removed by a plastic surgeon
                              in L.A.

        I wonder if he was then in the clutches
                        of the CIA/Intelligence robowashers
                fixing him up to be one of those "three month patsies"
                              or a killer
                              to whom Mnemosyne
                              is not a muse

In early March (March 4, to be exact)
J. Edgar Hoover updated the FBI's
                "Black Nationalists"
                Counterintelligence Program
                the one known now in disgust
                              as Cointelpro

At the time there were six (soon to be seven)
Cointelpros

They were very secret
not even revealed to the Attorney General
(especially not to Ramsey Clark)

Here's the list:
Cointelpro-Espionage
Conintelpro-New Left
(begun in May of '68)
Cointelpro-Disruption of White Hate Groups
Cointelpro-Communist Party, USA
Cointelpro-Counterintelligence and Special Ops
Cointelpro-Black Extremists/Black Nationalists
Cointelpro-Socialist Workers Party Disruption
(Hoover loathed the
scions of Trotsky)

Anyway, J. Edgar
spread abroad
to his secret police that March 4th
a document
against "black nationalist hate groups"
to "prevent the rise of a 'messiah'
who could unify and electrify the militant
black nationalist movement"

The hoov-doc
fingered MLK as a
"very real contender for this
position should he abandon his supposed
'obedience' to 'white liberal doctrines' and
embrace black nationalism."

Martin Luther King
wrote Hoov-boy in his March '68 directive
"has the necessary charisma to be a real threat
in this way."

Hoover revealed himself more paranoid than the
'noidest of the 'noids
sinking to the chasm
of MauMau-noia

as he wrote of the need to stave off
any coalition of black militant nationalists:

"An effective coalition of black nationalist groups
might be the first step
        toward real 'Mau Mau' in America,
the beginning of a a true black revolution."•

King's code name
        to the FBI
            was Zorro

March 4, I read with Allen Ginsberg, Ted Berrigan,
        Diane Di Prima and others at what was billed as a
BENEFIT FOR RECENTLY ARRESTED ANDREI CODRESCU•
            at the Poetry Project
                in the St. Mark's Church
(and on the 14th I gave a solo reading there)

A NIGHT OF TRUTH

Robert Bly's book of verse
The Light Around the Body
had won the National Book Award
and there was a big awards ceremony March 6
            in New York City

At first the bard was going to reject it
to protest the war

Then he decided to accept
on the condition he could make a statement
            longer than the usual
                brief bland quietudes.

The Book Award folk
        hestitatingly allowed it

so he created a speech, with the help of friends

35

<pre>
                    such as James & Anne Wright
                                and David Ray.
</pre>

<pre>
Bly faced
        the usual bifurcated crowd
                        on such an occasion in the late-'60s
Some were the tsk-tskers
        "Oh Gawd! What war?
                    This is an awards ceremony, not war!"
Others applauded his braveness
        and stamped their feet
                not long after he began:
</pre>

"I am uneasy at a ceremony emphasizing our current high state of culture. Cultural prizes, traditionally, put writers to sleep, and even the public. But we don't want to be asleep any more. Something has happened to me lately: every time I have glanced at a bookcase in the last few weeks, the books on killing of the Indians leap out into my hand. Reading a speech of Andrew Jackson's on the Indian question the other day—his Second Annual Message— I realized that he was the General Westmoreland of 1830..."

<pre>
And then,
        in a set of words
                that might have miffed
                        the mighty Harper and Row:
</pre>

"What have our universities done to end the war? Nothing. They actually help the war by their defense research. What has the book industry done to end the war? Nothing. What has my own publisher, Harper and Row, done to help end the war? Nothing....

"I respect the National Book Awards, and I respect the judges, and I thank them for their generosity. At the same time, I know I am speaking for many, many American poets when I ask this question: since we are murdering a culture in Vietnam at least fine as our own, have we the right to congratulate ourselves on our cultural magnificence? Isn't that out of place?

"You have given me an award for a book that has many poems in it against the war. I thank you for the award. As for the thousand

dollar check, I am turning it over to the draft–resistance movement,
specifically to the organization called the Resistance."

Bly handed the $1,000 check to Mike Kempton
                                        of the Resistance
                                                and then risked
            the indictment
                    served just weeks ago
                            to Dr. Spock, William Sloane Coffin
                            & other Resistance activists:

"I hereby counsel you
            as a young man
                    not to enter the United States Army,
        not under any curcumstances, and I ask you
                                            to use this money
        I am giving you to find and to counsel
        other young men,
                    urging them to defy the draft authorities—
            and not to destroy their spiritual lives
                            by participating in this war."

A glorious moment in 1968
            that reverberates
                    even unto the end of the century.

"There was silence in the hall
for a moment,"
            David Ignatow has written
"the silence of extreme tension
until, finally, a scattering of handclapping began."

            There was then
            an "uproar of talk
                    mixed with boos and cheers,"

        like the opening
                of a Chekhov play in the 1890s.

Bravery such as Bly's no doubt
                    miffed the creeps
                        in the CIA's Chaos program

because the CIA
        was trying to disrupt the Resistance movement
            as well as the Underground Press
                as detrimental
                        to the war

The CIA hated to be tabbed as
                        killers
By '68 many many
                thought they had killed JFK, and a
Dec 11, '67 memo by Howard J. Osborne CIA director of
Office of Security, complained that Eldridge Cleaver and
other black activists had
        dared to accuse the CIA of killing Patrice Lumumba in '61

(whose body, I once read, was carried around
                        in the trunk of the CIA station chief)

March 6
        about the time that Bly
                handed over the grand
                        to the Resistance
The Fugs, Country Joe and the Fish, Bob Fass, Paul Krassner
and Lightshow creators Joshua and Pablo
                did a benefit for
                        the Resistance at
the Anderson Theater on 2nd Avenue
        a place with a round rotating stage.

        Meanwhile,
                by early March it looked all triumph
                for the Festival of Life!

The first few weeks
Abbie Hoffman set up a bunch of prestigious committees
                        to plan the Fest
I was impressed at the time
                with their complexity
He had an intricate knowledge
                of the avant-garde N.Y. left•

Egoist males seemed to grab the spotlight
but there were a number of powerful women involved
                                    in the early Yippies:
Anita Hoffman, Sharon Krebs, Robin Morgan, Nancy Kurshan,
Kate Coleman, Judy Gumbo, and others

        For entertainers, the Yippies had Judy Collins, The Fugs,
        Arlo Guthrie, Pete Seeger, the Nitty Gritty Dirt Band, Richie
        Havens, Country Joe, Dick Gregory, Barbara Dane, Phil Ochs,
        Jim and Jean
                        but still no Dylan, Beatles or Stones.

Throughout the month
there were Saturday afternoon meetings at the Free University
at 20 East 14th Street near University Place

I'd taught a course there once
called Revolutionary Egyptology
            which had piqued the attention of the secret police

(Them commies, you know,
                will even use hieroglyphics
                                to spread the rev)

The Criminal and Subversives Section
                of the New York State Police
kept files, mainly on leftists and what they called
                            "subversive elements"

A study of the State Police a few years later
revealed that among the 1,000s of cards
                listing data on potential slime-commies
"One card noted that XXXXXXX was teaching a course in
                    'Revolutionary Egyptology.'"

        Yes, yes, I confess! I taught a course,
        heh heh, in Revolutionary Egyptology
        and loaned my fancy Sir Alan Gardiner
        Egyptian grammar
        to one of the students

and now take the opportunity
to plead for its return: o student of then
please mail my grammar
                to Edward Sanders
                Box 729
                Woodstock, N.Y. 12498.

The Saturday Yippie meetings at the Free U
were very, very crowded
There was much, much excitement and mirth
A brain-pleasing mixture
                of nonchalance and intensity

There were, of course, a good sample of factions
                whose souls seemed tattooed
                with the message, "I am unhappy"
A member of the group
known as the Motherfuckers
stood up
    and accused me
            of having a Swiss bank account

I laughed, knowing how close to the line
                Miriam and I lived
and defended myself as best I could—
It's true I'd suffered for a while the malady
                known as "limoanguia,"
that is,
the hunger to
be scooted around in limousines

but I remember being on the cover of *Life Magazine*
and not having enough for the rent

so if I'd known then that Brecht had had
                a Swiss account
I might have stood up and announced,
        well yes, that I had taken over
                Bertold's account
                        at Credit Suisse.

There is never any answer

to the snarl
"You don't care about
                    the suffering of the people
You only care about pleasure"

or the anger that crunches
                    the dry twigs
                            of left and right

                    A writer is never right enough
                    for the right
                    left enough for the left
                    pure enough for the pure
                    nor poor enough
                            for the poor of heart.

A story is told now and then
how once at Stanford in the '60s
a student heckled
                    the socialist Irving Howe
(one of the founders of *Dissent*)
over his lack of commitment
                            to the rev
That his fingers were sooty with Moloch's boot polish

Howe glanced over at the youth and replied,
"You know what you're going to be?
You're going to be a dentist."

                    The guy that heckled me at the Yippie meeting
                    later became a rancher in the Southwest.

                    Back in the fall of '67
                    Senator Eugene McCarthy
                    came to Robert Kennedy
                    to say that he was running for President
                            on an anti-war ticket
                                    if Kennedy were not

Kennedy felt that Vietnam
                    was a national tragedy

but believed that a challenge to Johnson
        would be political suicide

    There was a rush of support for McCarthy
    They called it the Clean for Gene phenomenon—
    as 5,000 people, clean shaven, eschewing beards
    and fresh of breath
            worked through New Hampshire
  in the earliest Democratic primary. Phil Ochs
       was among them
              singing all over the state

    On the 12th of March
    McCarthy stunned Johnson by getting
    42.2 percent vs. 49.4 for war.

Robert Kennedy thought McCarthy
      was weak on the poor & trodden
and talked with his friends incessantly
          to the click of the wingéd primaries
He knew, should he win, he might split the party
        and give it to Tricky
plus no incumbent had lost a renomination
        since Chester Arthur to James Blaine in '84

    The basic fact was that,
    for all his brilliance
       McCarthy lacked the manic metabolism
              required to win
    As I.F. Stone put it,
      "A certain cynicism and defeatism
      seem basic to the man."

March 13
    RFK was on Walter Cronkite's national news show
    and then after dinner
       Kennedy got on the phone with Democratic
              honchos around the country

    one of whom was Mayor Richard Daley of Chicago
    who urged him not to run

"I still wish the President would change his policy,"
said Daley. "You wouldn't feel this way."

Daley told Bobby he'd call Lyndon right away
            about setting up a high-level commission
            on Vietnam
                        to seek a wider road to peace

If Johnson would allow it
            then Kennedy would not run against him.

Shortly thereafter Daley called back,
according to the pro-Kennedy account,
and said that Johnson had told him,
"I'm all for this commission.
I'm waiting for Sorensen to give me the names."

Daley suggested that Kennedy contact
the newly sworn Secretary of Defense, Clark Clifford
                                    to move it ahead.

March 14
    Kennedy and Sorensen met with Clifford
            at the Pentagon at 11 am
                        to talk about who might sit on the commission

Clifford then met with Johnson at 4 pm
            pitched the list,
                    & Johnson said no

Clifford called Kennedy around 5
                        with the word..

SEED SYLLABLES FROM O

I had written Charles Olson in Gloucester
for a mantram we could chant in Chicago

I also asked Ed Dorn and d. a. levy.
It came from the chanting the Fugs and the Diggers

43

had done at the Pentagon
        "Out, Demons, Out! Out, Demons, Out!"
and the ceremony with Ginsberg at Senator McCarthy's grave

It was worth a try
        to see if a great bard's sung seed syllables
                        could help end the war.

The day President Johnson
        rejected Robert Kennedy's
                call for a national commission
                        on Vietnam
Olson called Avenue A
        and recited his mantram to Miriam:

        Plann'd in Creation, Arouse the Nation
        Blood is the Food of
        Those Gone Mad
        <u>*Blood is the Food of*</u>
        <u>*Those Gone Mad*</u>
        Blood is all over already This Nation,
        Plann'd in Creation, Arouse the Nation
        Blood is the Food of Those Gone Mad

    Olson then mailed us the Chant
            from Chicago
                on the way to deliver
                    his "Poetry & Truth" lectures
                            at Beloit College

He had his bard-eye
        on a big American problem:
The War Caste wanted blood
                (still does)

And the evening Olson
        chanted his mantram to Miriam
        there was a dinner party, 3 tables of 12,
                                at Hickory Hill—
        editors and publishers
                from the New York Press Association

At RFK's table sat *Village Voice* writer Jack Newfield
who "argued vigorously for legalization of marijuana
       and shocked the older guests by candidly admitting
       he smoked it himself with some frequency"
              in the words of
                     one of Ethel Kennedy's biographers.

       RFK overheard
       and wrote a note to Newfield
       Maybe you can talk about something else
       or you might cost me the nom
       and signed it Timothy Leary

It was during the Hickory Hill dinner
that Robert Francis Kennedy
              decided to run for President

March 15
       In the midst of big gold crisis
       The London gold market
       was closed at bequest of USA
              to stop huge gold sell-off
       it reopened April Fool's day•

                     This was the month
mal-mental'd, laissez-faire poverty-creator Milton Friedman
              had his "presidential address"
                     on
              "The Role of Monetary Policy"
       published in the *American Economic Review*

       He wanted the money supply increased 3%, say, per year,
       (with an unfettered market system
                     spitting the skulls of the poor
                                   to a dead-tired Tartaros)

On March 16
in a tiny place called My Lai 4
       the day began
              with each family lighting fires

in their yards
                and keeping pans of water boiling
while children went down to the river
to check the fish nets

        ee ee ee ee ee ee•

Then a group of helicopters landed
9 of them, dropped troops, & lifted off
                                to go get more
The three platoons of Charlie Company
                105 guys just three months in Nam—

The soldiers
        spread out
                racing to the bank of an irrigation ditch

A farmer
        raised his hands
                to show no weapon
They murdered him with a machine gun

More soldiers arrived
        They were shooting at any motion
but there was no return fire
                no VC
                just women, children, and older folk

        ee ee ee ee ee ee

They went through My Lai
        shooting pigs and cows
soldiers dispatching
        wounded Vietnamese with .45s
a woman with an unexploded M-79 grenade
                stuck in her stomach
fragmentation grenades tossed into huts
        —thank you Minneapolis Honeywell•

The soldiers went

what used to be known as berserk
One of them later
               talked of scalping and cutting out tongues

               ee ee ee ee ee ee

Medina
          was upset at the slowness
                         of moving on
Calley said
          there was a large group of civilians
                         slowing down the platoon
Medina said get rid of them
Calley then ordered all dead
Some complied, some cried, some refused
                         but many slaughtered

They herded the villagers
               to slaughter
Calley shoved a woman in a ditch
               and ordered a soldier to kill her
He refused
          but others did
mothers protecting babies
               people desperate
                         to slide beneath the already dead

          ee ee ee ee ee ee

Some took evil pleasure
               in the creation of gore
rape, slaughter, beheading,

One soldier
          bragged about, pants down,
                    penis exposed, trying to get a blow job
                              from a Vietnamese woman
               while threatening her child

A couple of soldiers
became what was horrifyingly known as "double veterans"

slang for raping then murdering
One solder raped with a rifle barrel
                    then pulled the trigger
There were scalpings
                tongue-cuttings—
a thread of evil
            that led forever to

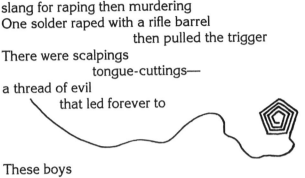

These boys
        soon to return
                to the U.S.
                        to be normal
                                tube-staring paycheckers.

                4 hours, 500.

            That night
            in the distance
            an old woman
                        grieved & keened so
            loudly & disturbingly that

            one of them
            lobbed a grenade
                        from an M-79 launcher
            Some others fired their M-16s, but

            she continued
            through the night,
            weeping & wailing

            eerily, the keen of ghosts,
            the lament of love
            the agony
                        of eternal separation

None of us knew about it for
                        at least a year and a half
till late '69
            after heroic work

by Seymour Hersh who published the story
                              during the second moon landing.

Finally, in the '80s, it took the truth of the tape recorder
                              and flying to the homes of prior soldiers
      to overwrite
            the clean visions of war
                              in Euripides, Homer, & the Pentagon Papers
      with Michael Bilton and Kevin Sim's
                  terrifying book
                        Four Hours in My Lai.

Robert Francis Kennedy announced for President
                                    on My Lai morn
      in the Senate Caucus Room
                  where his brother once declared

Ethel was there with 9 of their kids
Robert stood in a blue suit
                  and a gold PT-109 tieclasp
      reading his speech
                  from a black notebook typed in overlarge letters

and then he headed for
            NYC
                  to march in the St. Patrick's Day parade.

General Curtis LeMay
had retired from the airforce
                  and was living Bel Air, L.A.
The singer Eddie Fisher,
                  in his autobiography (page 340)
wrote about visiting LeMay
not long before Bobby announced his run:

            "Toward the end of our visit," wrote Fisher
            "I happened to mention that I was going to
            Bobby Kennedy's for his wife's telethon.

49

'Bobby Kennedy?' LeMay said without expression.
'He's going to be assassinated.'"

March 17
   Martin King was in L.A.
   to speak to the
   Democratic State Council
                in Anaheim

   & James Earl Ray
   filed a change-of-address card
   to general delivery
                Atlanta
   King's home city

ROBO

   At the risk of being accused a 'noid
   I think it's possible that Ray
   was a programmed assassin.
             In his book,
             The Search for the "Manchurian Candidate"
             John Marks interviewed a hypnosis expert,
             Milton Kline,
             a consultant for CIA hypnosis research,

             who claimed he could create a
                           assassin in six months.

THE POOR PEOPLE'S MARCH

The great Martin King
was leading the plans
             for a March on Washington
                    for April 22
which, had it been allowed to happen,
might have
            changed America

for the permanent better
(which is perhaps
        why he wasn't allowed)

The March on Washington
        was much more truly revolutionary
        than much of the dither of the New Left
It would have trembled America
        with its simple mode of
                "jobs, income and a decent life"

3,000 poor people
blacks, Puerto Ricans, whites, Indians, Mexicans
would go by caravan to D.C.
                pitch tents and sleep in them
& each day delegations
        would go to government departments

The numbers wd increase
                to great size
They'd stay camped out
        till there were results from the gov't

March 18
    RFK on a trip to Kansas
    at K State in Manhattan
                14,500 in the fieldhouse
        He told them how
        a huge struggle was tormenting America
        not for who would rule
                but for the heart of the nation—
        In the campaign months
                Americans would have to make
                decisions on what the nation will stand for,
                what kind of citizens?

"If you will give me your help, if you will give me your hand,
        I will work for you
                and we will have a new America."

    It was as if an explosion had occurred

Students surged, shouted, beat chairs together
and pressed toward the candidate
              in a hot high-metabolism moil of Yes
          till he finally got outside to stand in a convertible

That was the day
          Martin King broke into plans
                            for the Poor People's March
          & came to Memphis
                    to speak to the strikers

          Mayor Loeb had replaced them with scabs
          There'd been a protest march
          police ran over a woman's foot
          men rocked the car
          police then maced a number of ministers
          after which there were daily marches to city hall
                            & a boycott of downtown

          They asked King
                    to come and help
          as busy as he was with the March

          He spoke to a huge crowd
                    the night RFK was at K. State
          and said he would return
                      in a few days for a General Strike

          "I want a tremendous work stoppage,"
                              he told them
          "All of you, your families and children,
          will join me & I will lead you on a march
                        through the center of Memphis."

March 19
    Johnson signed a law eliminating the requirement
                    that 25% of U.S. currency be backed by gold.

      The Yippies held a press conference

at the Hotel Americana
    the day we began to end the gold standard
They'd acquired a professional p.r. guy, a volunteer,
who worked for Jimi Hendrix

It was a "slick" event in a function room
    with a shiny wooden rostrum
        with the words "Americana of New York"
            across the front
Tacked to the wall behind was a quilted banner
        sporting the word: YIPPIE

    "A Yippie is what happens
                to a hippie when a cop
        hits him over the head"
            the first speaker said

On hand were Allen Ginsberg, myself,
Paul Krassner, Judy Collins, Phil Ochs,
the producer Jacques Levy, Allan Katzman, Jerry Rubin—

"We are demanding the politics of the toe freaks
and kisses,"
        I chanted
"as opposed to the politics of the worm farm,
suicidal hysteria, slums, baby broil, and
the napalm drool cancer."

            Ginsberg unhooked his harmonium
            and sang Hare Krishna

I later found in my FBI files
        the following blurb
            on a heavily censored page:
"On March 19, 1968, Special Agents of the FBI observed a press
conference called by the YIP, held at the Americana Hotel, NYC, at
which ED SANDERS of the folk singers, the Fugs, stated that a
quarter of a million youth are going to Chicago to hold a Festival
of Life during the National Democratic Convention to demand
politics of ecstasy."

The March 20 headline in *Variety* was
the stixnixhixpix-ish
          "Yippie Music Theater
                    To Tune Up Viet Beefs
                              During Dems' Chi Conv"

The same day Joan Baez
          gave a concert and lecture
                    at Brooklyn College
                              for the Resistance

March 21
          an Israeli commando unit
                    attacked an Al Fatah center
                              in Karameh, Jordan

          the news of which no doubt upset
                    a young man in a small house in Pasadena
                              who was interested,
                                        as was James Earl Ray,
                                                  in hypnotism.

HYMN TO AVENUE A IN THE SPRING OF '68

> *Time held me green and dying*
> *Though I sang in my chains like the sea*
> —Dylan Thomas

Spring '68 was a very active time for me
& I was feeling good
          in the rebel zone
                    called the Lower East Side

In politics
I was glad that RFK was running
and didn't care
          that it would ebb
                    our Festival of Life

& I liked the way Peace Eye looked

with Spain's red and yellow sign
blazing on the boulevard
across from Tompkins Square Park

How temporary it all was
but for its part
in the mosaic
It froze there on the Avenue
for a few months
in a satisfying stasis
so that a stroll
from our house at 196 Avenue A
to Peace Eye at 147

was an anarcho-Bacchic Goof Strut
of contemplation & non-CIA chaos
the chaos of the first line of
Hesiod's *Theogony*

Ah, how I loved that Avenue of Goof
I loved the dripping faucets of Goof
I loved the hooting sax of Goof
smoking the hookah of Goof

Some called it lazy
Some called it spoof
Some called it crazy
but I called it Goof

Goof City
City of Flaming Teeth,
or maybe it was Eyes, for

Polis is
eyes

sang Olson the bard.

Our apartment at 196
was on the second floor
            above the Figlia Air Conditioning Co.
and just down the street
from Pee Wee's bar
            owned by blacks
            and very friendly to whites

Miriam had shoulder length blond hair
and flashed her pretty legs and shiny knees
            beneath the short short skirts of the time.
Deirdre was just under four
            and sometimes wore a little wrist bell
                        from the Psychedelicatessen

The house had one of those
            inner windows 'tween rooms
                        indicating it was old

(Inner windows were required
            in the 19th century
                        to spread light
                                    keep sickness down
            & to prevent depravity)

Our rooms were big
            almost like a loft
and our bedroom
            had windows
                        on the Avenue
and a marble fireplace

The kitchen had a porch
            we had to keep sealed with a police gate
            against the creepy-crawl of junkies

There was a big red wall in the middle room
with a golden Eye of Horus
            above a madras-topped floor mattress
and a vase with peacock feathers

On the opposite wall of the red room

was a shiny black floor-to-ceiling
                    set-up of shelves and cabinets
with a fine UHER stereo.

However, when Allen Ginsberg discovered
we didn't have a kitchen table
but ate with trays on the bed!

(the beats favored kitchen tables
with their zones
             of food and agitated talk)

he demanded we get one
so we went over to Elk's Trading Post
on Avenue B
and purchased a round oak table
Miriam stripped away
              a dozen layers of paint
down to its darkling grains
and ever thereafter
we carried its roundness
to whatever house the Fates
                    snipped and cut for us.

Miriam has a witty memory of the life-style nonchalance
                          on Avenue A.
Just as someone today might ask
                    "Do you mind if I smoke?"
In '68 they'd ask
                    "Do you mind if I shoot up?"

There was the sense
of being sensual all the time
                    without pressures.
A whole half-day
         in book store goof!
15 hours
      reading Kant
            in Kant-goof!
45 minutes
         in front of the peacock feather vase
               listening to Varèse & Beethoven

                                             at the same time!
Let's listen
          to every Coltrane cut again
                    in 'Trane-goof
Why not waste time
          for is not time itself
                    the biggest waster of them all?

Underneath the Goof, of course
lay the skree of weirdness, calamity and the secret police:

The Thérémin fill
          oo-
               oo-   oo-
                    oo-
in the Beach Boy's "Good Vibrations"

and the oo-ee-oo
          in Krzysztof Komeda's soundtrack
                    for *Rosemary's Baby*
were always there
          in the sounds of '68

(along with the throb of
          tall stacks of amplifiers,
                    the sizzle of napalm,
                         & the sky-groaning vowels of lycergica)

The secret police were always there also
                         like puking drunks in a phone booth
hung up on manipulation
looking for evidence of rubles
racist, pretty much right wing
                    & hating the left

     We were pitiably easy to monitor

     Miriam's mother would call Avenue A
     There'd be no ring
     and all of a sudden
               she could hear everything
                         in the room

(later, from reading my FBI files
I realized how closely surveilled we were,
I was shocked to learn that
the FBI at least twice
forwarded actual Fugs records
to the U.S. attorney
        "for prosecutive decision"
    to use the Bureau's own icy language)

How the Secret Police Bugged Your Talk in '68:
- leased lines
- phone tap
- room tap
- car tap

(A Panther attorney once told me
    the FBI had more than
        6,000,000 pages of transcripts
            of Panther conversations

            ai yi yi)

Here's a chart on the different types of bugs and taps
they used in '68:

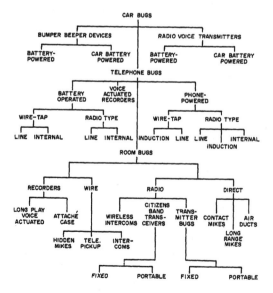

There were also what are known as "mail covers"
where a government agency
          gets the post office to copy
          the names and addresses
                    of mail you send and receive

and during the Vietnam war
          as many as 2,000,000 letters a year were
          examined by the CIA

The CIA invented a kind of oven
with which they could bake open
                    letters, copy, then reseal & send

The Agency had a "Watch List"
people whose mail
          was to be given
                    close scrutiny

which included such dangerous Americans
as John Steinbeck and Linus Pauling.

Was it Paul Goodman who said that
you can say anything you want in America
                    as long as it doesn't have an impact?

March 22
     General William Westmoreland was chosen
                    the Army Chief of Staff
               after running the forces in 'Nam

Meanwhile, in March, the military
               got ready
                    for stern streets
                         with their secret "Cable Splicer" maneuvers.

     The poet Bob Kaufman
               had a book once called
                    "Does the Secret Mind Whisper?"

In '68 the white power noise
                of the secret mind
                        hissed on our phone lines
with orders to monitor
the concept of armed blacks from ghettos
combining with politicized hippies, tipi-heads,
                        partisans of music
                                & the underground press
                (stirred up by rubles & commies)

to wreak fire
        on the capitalist safety zones.

The first Cable Splicer exercise was in March of '68
(They were held each year through '73
                in Arizona, California, Oregon and Washington)
Over 1,000 persons participated in the '68 Cable Splicer exercise.
State, county and local law enforcement from six states, plus National
Guard personnel and U.S. Army advisors

The Cable Splicer exercises
        formed a "regional subplan" for a DOD program codenamed
                "Garden Plot"

to be used in coping with large-scale civil disturbances
                (such as the one they helped stir up in Chicago).

That Thing Called Yip-In

The Yippies called for an early spring Yip-In
                at Midnight, Friday, March 22
                        in the cavernous Grand Central Station
                                on 42nd Street

        The Yip-In, as I recall,
        was the concept of Keith Lampe
                who wanted a celebration
                to shake off the snowy winter
                        of the garbage strike

        The Yippie flier had a map of Grand Central Station,

with the text:
     "BRING:
          BELLS, FLOWERS BEADS,
          KAZOOS, MUSIC, FM, RADIOS (TO WBAI)
            PILLOWS, EATS,
              LOVE AND
               PEACE"

The plan was to party all night
then dance forth at dawn like bassarids
     up to the Sheep Meadow in Central Park
          "to YIP up the sun" •

     The Yippies still trailed
          a swirl of good will
   so the New York FM rock stations
          gave the Yip-In many free plugs
   with the result
      the Station was packed
          with 6,000 curious and querulous youth.

The elegant information booth
      with its familiar round clock
         in the station's center

was aswarm with loitering youth
      like bees on a tree branch

The tiny faction known as the Motherfuckers
were on hand
     bent on violence
One of them raised a banner festooned with the cop-inciting words,
        UP AGAINST THE WALL, MOTHERFUCKER

and at 1 AM firecrackers and cherry bombs exploded
while a querl-youth tore the hands from the clock

That's when the cops began to club

Abbie asked an aide to Mayor Lindsay
if he could use the P.A.
     to calm the crowd

> but the aide said no

When the Tactical Patrol Force
(dreaded by demonstrators
                as much as
            the ancient Athenians
            feared their Scythian policemen)

moved in
        with whacking billies
there was NO ROOM TO MOVE
whack
            stick-butt face
                    whack

            A cop grabbed Ron Shea, 22, from
            behind, as he stood in the terminal
            and ran him toward the exit doors
            on 42nd street

            The four doors in the middle
            were open
            the door on the right was closed
            The cop changed shove–direction
            and mashed Shea into
                    the closed door's glass

            He threw up his hands
            to save his face

            but wrists were slashed
            an artery severed
            and tendons in both hands severed

I was recording at Impact Sound
                    on the next Fugs album
and arrived late.•

I came into Grand Central
There was broken glass

and policemen holding clubs

One of the first friends I saw
was young *Village Voice* reporter Don McNeill
Runnels of blood, not yet congealed
were dripping down his face
He was very angry
The cops had smashed him too
            through a plate glass door

Uh oh,   👓   eyes of reproach!

He was angry at the Yippies
            (and me as well)
for their lack of planning
They had no bullhorn,
had done no negotiations Quaker/CNVA style• with
The New York Central railroad
                  and the police.

            It was the age old problem of the Left:
                  Long on shouts
                  Short on Shinola

I shuddered at the eyes of reproach
from the rising young writer
who'd come to New York
            from the University of Washington
for a "Junior Year in Washington Square"
dropped out, and in late '65 was a volunteer at Peace Eye
helping with the Committee to Legalize Marijuana
then starting to work for the *Voice*
            where he covered the counterculture

            It was first of many many eyes of reproach
            for associating with the Yippies.

New York Times put the Yip-In on the front page
with a photo showing a gnarl of youth
            sitting on the information center
and a querl-kid

pulling off the clock hands
above an article
on the "politicization" of hippie

(If this poem had a sound track
there'd be the snipping sounds
of secret police agencies
the FBI, CIA, ONI, NSA, NY Red Squad
et alia multa
clipping *The New York Times*
that morning)

The day after the Yip-In
Arthur Greenspan wrote in the *New York Post*
"Ed Sanders charged that Tactical Patrol Force
officers during Friday's fracas 'when away from
the people who control them acted like mad
dogs.' He said police acted like a 'Grade B
Indian movie,' and said, 'they're terrorizing kids,
they're terrorizing people with long hair.'"

It didn't bode well for Chicago
If they threw people through doors
for tearing off clock hands
what would they do
to 500,000
making love
in Grant Park?

The night of the Yip-In
James Earl Ray was in a motel in Selma
Martin Luther King was supposed to stay in town that night
but instead stayed 30 miles away

The day after the Yip-in
a bunch of Yippies flew to the midwest
for a meeting of the Mobilization to End the War
in Vietnam (everywhere called the Mobe)
and then to Chicago
to meet with Mayor Daley's staff

                    (the mayor himself
                          made himself scarce)
In a climate of frolic & satire
The Yippies presented a formal request
                    for a million person freak-out space,
                          grope zone, and lifestyle encampment

March 25–29
    Monday, Wednesday, Friday
                the bard Charles Olson
    gave the lectures called *Poetry and Truth*
    at Beloit College in Wisconsin

    I was grateful, reading them later,
    that he had expounded in Beloit
    in fairly understandable detail,
    on the terms "topos, typos and tropos"
    from his great essay on poetics
                          Projective Verse.

For the Beloit lectures
        in early March
                Olson wrote three short, exquisite poems

two of which ever since
    I have read over and over
                as numinal text

    The first I keep in my writing studio
            on the wall
                    neath the Endymion medal from Mardi Gras
    the one beginning,
            "an actual earth of value to
            construct one..."

and the "Beloved Lake" poem
beginning,
            "Wholly absorbed
                into my own conduits to
                an innner nature or subterranean lake..."

While Olson was delivering his
                    lectures in Beloit
there were three days of performances at the Electric Circus
                    a popular club of the time
                              on St. Mark's Place
billed "3 Ring Yippie"
to raise money
          for the Festival of life

March 26: Judy Collins, Blood, Sweat & Tears
      Taj Mahal, Elephant's Memory

March 27:
      The United States of America
            Dave Van Ronk
                  Taj Mahal

March 28:
      Blood, Sweat & Tears
            The United States of America
                  The Stone Ponies
            Jimmy Collier & Rev. Kirkpatrick

Somewhere about now
            in the time-flow
Judy Collins had a dispute with Abbie and Jerry
                        and dropped away

March 26
      an open letter to Richard Daley
            and park commissioner William McFetridge:

"Thousands of young Americans, possibly upwards of 500,000, will be coming to Chicago this summer from August 25 to August 30 for a national youth festival—a celebration of life and an affirmation of man and community.

"The festival will be held in Grant Park, and will last continuously for the week....Response to the Festival of Life, also called the Yippie festival, has been overwhelming....

"Because of the other affair being held simultaneously with our festival, and because of the enormous number of people expected, those attending the festival will need to sleep in the park. We are urging them to bring sleeping bags, blankets and tents.

"We are asking the city to cooperate in providing portable sanitation units. In addition, our emphasis will be on food sharing and we will ask the Health Department to cooperate with us in the setting up of kitchens in the park."

                    it was signed
                         "For fun and freedom"

with Paul Krassner, Jerry Rubin, Abbie Hoffman, Jim Fouratt, among those putting pen to the bottom.

                    Many many times
                    as the decades have trickled past
                    I've asked myself why I,
                    a pacifist, bard, and Social Democrat
                    ever associated with
                              the violent-hearted core of the Yippies.

          I think it's because
          of the evil I perceived
          going on in Vietnam
                    To me the use of napalm and
                    fragmentation bombs
                              sank down to the gutter of Hitler

& I wanted very much
              to believe in the Yippies
just as I had come to believe
              in Olson and Sappho
in Greek lyric poetry
in "Howl"
          & the early Joan Baez records

68

I wanted the level of belief
          I gave to a work of art

Jerry was honest
He said to me he wanted a revolution
                    like that in Cuba
"We have to make it happen here,"
                         he told me

The closest Abbie
          came to calling for a direct rev
          (in my direct experience)
          was talking about "tossing it up for grabs"

               (The problem with throwing it up for grabs
                is Grabs likes to throw too)

As for Jerry,
          after a while
               a few of us began
                         to call him Bloodbath Rubin
because it was obvious
               he was hot for whacked heads and violence

          He said, in an issue of *RAT* in early March,
               "The Democrats will probably have to travel from
               hotel to convention hall by helicopter. Johnson
               will be nominated under military guard, under the
               protection of army bayonets. Even if Chicago does
               not burn, the mass paranoia and guilt of the
               government will force them to bring thousands of
               troops, and the more troops, the better the
               theater."

     Whatever would come
     Abbie & Jerry (and Jim Fouratt)
     had a lot of credit
                    built up in the counterculture
                    for tossing the money onto the stock exchange floor
               (The image of stockbrokers groveling to their

knees to grab it was an anecdote
                    chortled o'er across the land)
& then when they were tossed out
for burning some greenbacks
                    on the stock market steps

An actual dollar bill burned outside the
Stock Exchange late in the Summer of Love, '67

Many New Leftists
questioned the paradigm
            of luring youth to Chi
            giving them rock
                        and lots of dope
            then saying, in effect,
                        "time to face bayonets now
                        so that you'll become
                        revolutionaries
                                    in the bad experience

            like Lenin after the hanging
                        of his brother in 1880"

It was easy to chip away at Yippie
There was no mass base
            although in America a mass base is what a
                        sit-com has

Early in *Revolution for the Hell of It*
Hoffman quotes
            his August '67 speech
"Whoever hesitates while waiting for ideas to triumph

among the masses before initiating revolutionary
action will never be a revolutionary."

LSD AND THE '68 REV'S

Looking back in hindsight
　　I am aware how much LSD played a role
as in the first paragraph of the
　　　book Abbie Hoffman was writing in '68
　　　　　　"Once one has experienced LSD...one realizes that
　　　　　　action is the only reality."

　　The Mark of Acid
　　　　　　was stamped on the time

　　LSD had not long ago
　　　　　　　　been made illegal
　　and many were
　　　　　　in a defiant mood

　　R. Crumb has talked about
　　how acid changed his art
　　　　　　　　—helped him expand his drawing

　　Acid changed those
　　　　　　whose changes
　　　　　　had led them to tab their tongues

COLUMBIA

Meanwhile the great trouble
at Columbia University began
　　　　　　late in March

On the 27th a student named Mark Rudd led
　　　　　　a hundred-person delegation in to Low Library
　　　　　　(the administration building)
　　　　　　　　with a petition against the
　　　　　　　　Institute for Defense Analysis
　　　　　　　　one of those how-to-kill-or control-'em better
　　　　　　　　intellectual war tanks

which had a close relationship with Columbia
and did research, for example,
on something called "riot control"

March 27
James Earl Ray purchased a rifle in Birmingham
then exchanged it the next day for a Remington 30.06
with a telescopic sight

March 28
King flew from New York
where he'd been on a fundraising tour with Harry Belafonte
to Memphis
to lead the march to city hall
from the Clayborn Temple A.M.E. church

His plane was over an hour late
and the huge crowd
had already begun to flow

There were a handful intent on looting
and the '68 antagonisms
—stirred in part by the
FBI and CIA—
'tween Black Power violence
& Nonviolent Direct Action
broke forth.

King noted the disarray,
people crowding the sidewalk
more of a swell than a march
but nevertheless got out of his car
linked arms with ministers
and began the march
singing "We Shall Overcome"
headed toward City Hall

Then there was the sound of windows breaking
from the punch of poster staves
& the grabbing of American largesse
It was decided that King

would abandon the march, and police
escorted him to the Riverfront Hotel
(as opposed to his usual place-of-stay,
the black-owned Lorraine Motel)

The police then donned gas masks
crushed the march with
tear gas, mace and clubs

Many were high school kids
who fought back
the police becoming hysterical,
beating bystanders and marchers
and a young man was killed

Mayor Loeb called a 7 pm curfew
The governor called in 4,000 federal troops

King grieved
He felt guilty perhaps
& his entire
Poor People's March on Washington
coming up in April
was threatened

March 28
James Wright and Richard Howard
read poetry
and discussed "What Has Been Happening
in American Poetry Since World War II"
at Stuyvesant High School,
NYC

March 29
King slept exhausted for the night
awakened
in the shift of grace
8 hours can bring, then
announced to the press a
big march April 5, Friday
in Memphis

after which he flew back to Atlanta
                         for a staff meeting at his church
        then Sunday to D.C. to preach at the Washington Cathedral.

At the end of March
        Johnson was telling people he would not
             win any of the upcoming primaries:
             Wisconsin, Indiana, Nebraska, Oregon, Calif.

  and so on April Fool's eve
        Johnson abdicated
                     in a television talk to the nation

        He lifted the crow's feet that spread
        out from his eyes to his dangling ears
                             in a goodbye smile

        McCarthy was winding up campaign in Wisconsin
        Robert Kennedy was returning from his
                             first campaign trip
        and was told when the plane landed
                             at JFK
        with a large group of fans
                             by the exit ramp

    That night Kennedy
         sent Johnson
             a telegram
                 calling his no-run decision
                         "truly magnanimous"
    (Sorenson, Schlesinger, Walinsky, RFK, and
    others helped write it)

April 1
    RFK toured N.J. and then to Pennsylvania
    where he said, to students,
    "Stopping the bombing must be part
    of a coordinated plan.... The first thing we must recognize is that
    we will have to negotiate with the NLF. It is silly for our gov't
    to act as if the NLF does not exist."

No doubt the War Caste
winced in its secret rooms
at this April surprise

The next day
Eugene McCarthy won 57.6% in Wisconsin Dem Primary,
vs Johnson 35.4

That was the week
there was a big Draft Card Return in Boston
sponsored by the Resistance

April 3
Not wanting his youth to fall to
rock and roll and thrills
Castro, according to a Reuters dispatch,
on April 3, banned beards, long hair and tight pants
at Havana U

the same day a
a referendum for immediate ceasefire and troop withdrawal
was defeated in Madison 27,533 to 20,679

April 3
King flew to Memphis from Atlanta
and checked into the Lorraine Motel
where he usually stayed

About noon a black detective
went to a back room at a nearby fire station
and taped a newspaper to a window
that looked out upon the 3rd floor balcony
of the Lorraine (King's room)

He cut out holes in the newspaper
then put his binoculars up against them
and jotted the license plates
and names of visitors
and, as much as possible,
who did what.

The detective was joined by another black patrolman
                        between them they could i.d.
                        virtually all the
                                    black activists in Memphis

The march on city hall,
            called for April 5,
                    was moved to the 8th
                            to wait for supporters from across the USA

King paused
            for photographs
                    on the balcony
—maybe giving the kill team an idea

In the early evening— not long after 7—
            James Earl Ray
                in role as Eric Starvo Galt
                            checked into the New Rebel Motel in
                                    Memphis

There was a wild spring rain
            that thrummed upon the metal roof
                    of the Masonic Temple

Two thousand supporters
applauded wildly
            when Martin King came up the steps to the podium

He had an intense awareness
                    of the danger
as he gave out his gravely, high pitched, blues-chant
                                voice of the Numina:

"And some began to talk about the threats that were out,
of what would happen to me
                    from some of our sick white brothers…
Well, I don't know what will happen now.
We've got some difficult days ahead.
But it really doesn't matter with me now.

76

Because I've been to the mountaintop!"

There was great applause; thunder outside; lightning.

"And I don't mind. Like anybody I would like to live...a long life.
Longevity has its place. But I'm not concerned about that now....
I just want to do God's will! And He's allowed me to go up to the
mountain... And I've looked over, and I've seen the Promised land.
I may not get there with you, but I want you to know, tonight,
that we as a people will get to the Promised land!
So, I'm happy tonight. I'm not worried about anything.
I'm not fearing any man!
     Mine eyes have seen the glory of the coming of the Lord!"

    Then he turned away from the mike of prophecy
          drained from the thanatopsis
        & left the podium
      a moment that many have watched
            over the years
               with bitter regret.

At Riverside Church on April 4, '67
King had said, "The greatest
          purveyor of violence
             in the world today—
       my own government."

Hoover had sent a "secret" report,
one of a continuing stream, to the White House on
4-19-67, with the language:
     "Based on King's recent
     activities and public utterances,
     it is clear that he is an instrument
     in the hands of subversive forces
     seeking to undermine our nation."

By early '68, as we have seen,
Hoovy-boy was afraid of the rise
         of King in a Black Messiah mode
and it occurs to me
    thirty years later

that the gents of CIA Chaos
and Hoover's right wing array

might have actually believed King
                    might soon be seen as a Messiah
(though King was much too guilt ridden
when you read his biographies
ever to have declared himself the M)

Just a few weeks before the shooting
Hoover prepared a lengthy report on King
his opposition to the war
the threat of the Poor People's Campaign
his sex life,
            including the Willard Hotel
                    "two day, drunken sex orgy "
                            in the Bureau's kind words

& a section called "King's Mistress,"
            the wife of a California dentist
                    they surveilled him seeing.

        There was a big campaign
        to get King to call off the Poor People's Campaign
                            It didn't work

You can hear the chant in the halls of robokill:
        "He won't call off the PPC
        He's a Messiah
        An antiwar traitor
        One of his advisors is a commie
        He's a sexcrazed burrhead
                    (Hoover called him a burrhead)
        He's on the rise
        Nothing can stop him
        Hey, let's kill him"

On April 4 at 3:15 p.m.
    James Earl Ray, using the name Willard•
            checked into a rooming house

                                  whose back side
                                  faced King's motel

       —the bathroom in the hallway had a view
                       of King's door
                                  and the balcony
                                            on the third floor

              The window was opened
                       a few inches
                                  & apparently by standing in the bathtub
              someone could fire a rifle
                                            directly toward the area
                                  of King's room

4:00 p.m.
              Ray drove to a gun shop
                       in his white Mustang with Alabama plates
                       to purchase some binoculars

Right around then
                       the police pulled the two black firemen from
                       the firehouse by the Lorraine
                       and also ordered the two black police surveillors
                                                       out of the building

5:40 p.m.
              King and Abernathy came out of Rm 201 and went up
              the steps to Rm 306

Just before 6
         King came out onto the balcony

His associates were arrayed down below
                    in the courtyard
with a limousine on loan from a
                         local black funeral home

He stood on the balcony
                  for a minute or two
then back into his room
Abernathy wanted to put on aftershave lotion
King said he'd wait for him on the balcony
where he chatted with people,
                    including young Jesse Jackson of Chicago

It was just the moment
           they all prepared to walk down
                    the iron-edged steps

              then a shot
                    and King fell down
                           blood spurting from his jaw

           Certain types of secrets
           are possible to keep
           The Eleusinian Mysteries
           were not betrayed
                    for 1,000s of years

        An FBI agent in a car
                    hearing the news on the radio
              shouted, "We finally got the son of a bitch!"

           RFK's chartered plane
           was just on its way
                         from Muncie to Indianapolis
           a reporter rushed up the aisle
                              with the horror

     They apparently didn't think
              to ask the pilot to radio ahead

so when the plane landed
    RFK aide Fred Dutton
        sprinted to airport security
            to confirm it
The motorcade went to the rally
Kennedy spoke at once
      to the festive crowd
        many of them black

"I have bad news for you
for all of our fellow citizens
and people who love peace all over the world
and that is that Martin Luther King was shot and killed tonight"

      Kennedy spoke movingly and spontaneously
      including his famous quote from Aeschylus

"My favorite poet was Aeschylus. He wrote: 'In our sleep,
pain which cannot forget falls drop by drop upon the heart
until, in our own despair, against our will, comes wisdom
through the awful grace of God.'"

I remembered so intensely
      standing beneath a big tall elm
          by the Lincoln Memorial
that hot day in August '63

to hear King give his "I Have a Dream"
& now
    I hated the guy that killed him

    though nothing the repressionists
        would do
           by King day
    surprised me.

Jimi Hendrix, Buddy Guy and B.B. King
      played a club in the Village
        the weeping night of King•
They stood on the stage together
in the timeless agony of genius blues

It had the "threinos"
                of a weeping chorus
                        in a Greek tragedy
                (let's say the *ee ee* of the chorus
                        at the end of *Trojan Women*)

The club passed the hat
        for King's Southern Christian Leadership Conference
                and Jimi put in a check for $5,000.

That night too the beautiful Bernadine Dohrn
                a graduate of University of Chicago Law
                        working for the National Lawyers Guild
                                & very active in SDS
                                        changed into her demonstration attire
                                pants and loose clothing
and went up to Times Square,
                weeping for King
She'd worked with him in Chicago

There was a demonstration
                They ripped down signs,
                        broke windows
        Some kids trashed a jewelry store

Even as she wept
                she felt the fierce hands of Bellona
                        goddess of war

These were months
in which a few young and quick
became radicals, then socialists
and even communists
                        in quickened time

who saw the need
for revolution now
                BY ANY MEANS NECESSARY.•

On April 5
    A brown envelope come to 696 E. Howard St
                                in Pasadena
    for Sirhan Sirhan, from the Argonaut Insurance Co.
                    settlement at last for the '66 fall from a horse
    He'd expected $2,000. It was $1705

THE SHOVE OF BACCHUS

Bacchus, as ever,
                pushed into the Grief
and the Fugs flew the day after King to Cinncinati
for an arts festival

I remember how someone
                  at Frank O'Hara's funeral
asked if there was a party afterwards

              Sitting next to me on the plane was
              a young woman
              who claimed she was returning
              from a tour as a hetaira for
                      one of Ohio's senators.

For a city that
                later persecuted Mapplethorpe
there was a glut of fun in Cinncinati

for instance, a party in our motel
where a Fug (not I!) frolicked with a fan
after which they watched a Mexican vampire movie
while his toe was
              moving gently
                  in and out of the entrance
                        of Venus.

Meanwhile, the same night
the bullet at the Lorraine
seemed to many

the full flaring signal
            that right wing racist vomit
                        had won

The sword stabbed blacks
            in their hoping hearts
& big riots began in D.C., Baltimore, Chicago
                        Detroit, Boston
                            and 125 other places
where 46 died
        with over 20,000 arrested
                    55,000 troops sent to quell
                stats that do not tell the pain

        In Chicago, for instance,
        5,000 fed troops and 6,700 Illinois National Guardsmen
                were dispatched to assist police
        Mayor Richard Daley soon
        criticized the Chicago PD
        "for having failed to take more aggressive action when
            the riot started."

April 6
        There was a gun fight in Oakland
                'tween Black Panthers
                    and police

        & a 17 year old, Bobby Hutton, was killed
        The Panther
                Minister of Information Eldridge Cleaver and
                    Panther Warren Wells were wounded
        Two policemen also hurt
        8 Panthers, including Cleaver, arrested
        Cleaver ultimately freed on 50K bail
        (he had been paroled in '68 after serving 9 of 14 for
                    '58 Calif conviction of assault with intent to kill)

April 8
        Jorge Luis Borges
                    read poetry
                        at the 92nd Street Y

April 9
   Gen. Creighton Abrams
            became U.S. Commander in Nam
                     & the napalm, defoliation,
                     fragmentation bombs
                              evil'd onward.

      The stock market didn't mind the King hit
      or the riots
                Maybe it liked Johnson gone
                         and uppity King erased
                the gold crisis "averted"
                when on April 10
                         the volume of shares traded
                was the greatest since the market crash of '29

                and Marianne Moore
                         tossed out the first pitch at Yankee Stadium.

April 11 An Ominous Bill from the Republocrats

      Martin King's killing
                (and the riots of grief)
      sped up passage of the 1968 Civil Rights Act
                to ban racial discrimination in the sale or rental of
      housing.
                The bill was signed today

      Congress slid into the Act what they called the
                "Rap Brown amendment"
                         making it a crime to cross state lines
                         "with the intent to incite, organize, promote,
                              encourage, participate in and carry on a riot."

Meanwhile, on Rap Brown day
         25 Yippies sat in at City Hall
                         to get a permit for the Central Park
                Yip-Out on Easter Sunday

                It worked. Lindsay official Sid Davidoff

negotiated with Abbie et al
and
with Davidoff agreeing to send their requests for
Sheep Meadow to Parks Commissioner Heckscher.
Davidoff said he'd return in an hour.
He did.
Permission was granted.

And in Germany on April 11
There was the attempted rub-out of Rudi Dutschke,
of the Socialist Students' League.

This brought about huge student demonstrations
throughout West Germany.

As in the U.S. the right took advantage
of public dislike
of protests in the street
and so in the April 28 elections the
right-wing National Democratic Party of Germany
(Nationaldemokratische Partei Deutschlands, or NFD)
in the state elections in Baden-Wurtenberg
made a leap in the vote count

April 11 in Lansing
a report to Kennedy's security
of a rifle on a roof
An aide
came into Kennedy's room
and pulled the curtain
Kennedy, getting into a clean shirt,
"Don't close them. If they're
going to shoot
they'll shoot."

Then the car to take him out
was brought to the basement
Bobbie was miffed
"What's the car doing down here?"

"We have a report—maybe serious."

"Don't ever do that. We always
get into the car in public.
We're not going to start ducking
                                        now."

April 15
    Richard Daley announced that from now on
    police would "shoot to kill" arsonists and "shoot to maim" looters.
    Tactless, tasteless, and out of sync
                        with the sounds of what was needed

    But it was real
                    and it rhymed with a streak of meanness
                                        in the populace

    Daley picked up massive ink
                    for the "shoot to kill"
            The Civil Rights movement
                        groaned but, after King,
                                    probably expected anything.

It's not easy, even 30 years later,
to track the role of
Military Intelligence
            in the upcoming Chicago mess

    There was an Army Unit
                    outside Chicago
            in suburban Evanston
                        called the 113th Military Intelligence Group

    that worked with a right wing group called the Legion of Justice
    to plant bugs in groups such as the
                        American Friends Service Committee

    and to disrupt anti-war groups

This supposedly happened from '69 through '71
but didn't it happen too in '68?

The 113th Military Intelligence group
supplied the Legion of Justice
             with mace, surveillance devices, and money
& the Legion planted bugs for Mil-Int
                  —it was a right wing swap meet.

There was a kind of "survnoia" in the era:
        Military-Intelligence agents
                   on duty to preserve western culture
        nodded in quiet dread
             as they copied down the
                        dreadful out-of-state license plates

             at the demo planning meeting. •

It was around this time a few of us
                        flew again to Chicago
I paid for Rubin and maybe Abbie
                   I smiled seeing them
             in the youth fare line
                             getting their tickets
We met with Dick Gregory
who was running for President
                   with Mark Lane
                   for a party called
                   Independents of America

Up to then we'd said
we were doing the Festival of Life in Grant Park
Gregory suggested we
                    do it instead at Lincoln Park
              because it was used by blacks
                          whereas Grant was almost totally a white-zone
We agreed
              and Lincoln thereafter
                          was our place.

A GOOD STABLE BAND

By the spring of '68
              the Fugs finally put together a stable and excellent band
       I wanted an ensemble that
                          could play outdoors
                                    in front of thousands
                                              and deliver thrills

April 11 The Fugs flew to Denver
                    to play a version of the Avalon Ballroom
                                        that had opened there
       then we flew the next day to San Francisco
                          to play the main Avalon
                                        April 12, 13, 14
       Jim Morrison was backstage one night
       in his snake skin pants
       swigging from a Jim Beam bottle
              a bit too wasted to ask him
                          to sing in Chicago

We stayed in S.F. till the 17th
with a few extra days to party

Charles Olson was in town
              after the Beloit lectures
                          for two weeks
                    (He had a gig to experiment with other poets
                                        in the new medium of video)

       staying with editor/publisher Don Allen

on the pull-out sofa in his apartment on Jones Street
(Allen's Four Season Foundation would publish
Poetry and Truth
several years later)

One morning I visited Janis Joplin
who excitedly showed me a packet of seeds
Richard Brautigan had given her
with a poem glued to the side

I told her that the great Charles Olson was in town
and would she like to meet him?

I thought maybe Olson could write some songs for her
and, well, both were single
maybe there could be some eros
between bard and blues

We went to a restaurant
in Chinatown
and since Don Allen was the
famous editor of *New American Poets*
and the *Evergreen Review*
the party was paid for by Grove Press!

Afterwards
we crowded into a booth at Gino and Carlo's
in North Beach

Olson was talking about Sutter's Mill
and the word "Donner Party"
entered the quick flow of his words
Around then Janis went to the back
to shoot pool

and my plans for
a blues/bard romance
were racked up on the green

April 17
The Fugs flew to Los Angeles

and stayed once again at Sandy Koufax' Tropicana
                    at 8585 Santa Monica Boulevard
                just a few blocks from the Troubadour Bar

During our two weeks in L.A.
the jukeboxes in barland were singing
the seething/soothing of
                Leonard Cohen's "Suzanne."

    We performed on the 19th and 20th
    at the Cheetah, a place built on piers
                    on the beach in Venice
    It was like playing Coney Island
    There seemed to be a glut
                    of bikers backstage
    Some of the Straight Satans
                    for instance, who lived nearby

    Janis came to one of the gigs
    and partied at the Tropicana the next several days
    At 2 AM she decided to take a swim
    I watched from the balcony
    She was topless
            & at first the place was desolate
    but then, in minutes, the poolsides came awake!
    as if it were daytime
            a dogwalker standing by the bougainvillea
                    people holding drinks
                            and chatting with vigor

The front desk rang my room.
"Mr. Sanders, I'm sorry
but the Fugs will have to
leave if Miss Joplin
continues
        to swim
            bare breasted"

POSSIBLE CAREER MISTAKE

I used to take a cab over the Hollywood Hills
and down into the San Fernando Valley to Burbank
to visit Warner/Reprise
                    the Fugs recording label

I'd talked with execs at Reprise
about a movie idea I had
starring Jimi Hendrix and Janis Joplin

They'd be marooned together
on a Mississippi river boat
                    in a flood

They'd be romantically involved,
                    as they say,
and they'd sing together

It was a good idea
Just the concept of Janis & Jimi
singing on the same track
            their voices woven together
                        or maybe in call and response
with Jimi's genius guitar
would have been a marvel

                    I could hear
                    her voice
                        & his guitar & voice
                    make hieroglyphics
                    in my Egyptian
                            mind

            At the Warner Brothers complex
            I was introduced to Ted Ashley
            of the Ashley Famous Agency
            and when the Fugs returned to New York
            I got a call from Warner Brothers
            They wanted to do it!

I'd get my own office and secretary
                                but I'd have to move to L.A.

I should have done it
but, well, I was working hard on
                    the new album at Alderson's studio
I'd just reopened Peace Eye on Avenue A

so I turned it down.

As for the Fugs
for years I had accepted
            the strange wisdom
that a band had to have both a rhythm guitarist
AND a lead guitarist

When we'd gone to California in February
our lead guitarist Danny Kootch
announced he was leaving
                    and moving to L.A.

(where he ultimately formed a songwriting team
with Don Henley of the Eagles)

After Kootch left
we did quite well with Ken Pine
            as our single scorching guitarist

In another change, we copied the Mothers of Invention
and used two drummers—adding Bob Mason

It caused a bit of friction with Weaver at first
but it freed him
        to do his brilliant routines
                            & stride the stage.

While we were in L.A.
our bass player Charlie Larkey
met and fell in love with the songwriter/performer Carole King

and announced that he too
                   was leaving the Fugs
though he'd stay through our upcoming
Scandinavian tour

(We replaced him with Bill Wolf,
with a fine harmony voice
after which for the final months of the
Fugs' first incarnation we stayed the same:
Pine, Mason, Wolf, Weaver, Kupferberg, and myself)

          We had a memorable photo shoot
          for our album cover
          at the Warner Brothers movie lot in Burbank

          We had our pick of costumes
          from the Warner Brothers wardrobe department
          We ordered anything we wanted
                             from movies we'd seen

          Larkey, for example,
          perhaps under the influence of Carole King,
          ordered the attire of a 19th century Viennese fop

          Weaver was transformed into a horn-headed
                             9th century berserker

Ronald Reagan was then the right wing governor
                             of California

(and we would have bet big money
                  in the spring of '68
                  he'd never be president)

so I ordered Reagan's "Win just one for the Gipper"
football uniform from *Knute Rockne: All-American*
and a tuxedo from a Fred Astaire–Ginger Rogers movie
plus an Errol Flynn D'Artagnon renaissance
                  puff sleeved outfit
                             with a sword.

We went to some Warner Brothers sets
The place where they shot the TV series "F Troop"
                              with its famous falling tower
and to the sets of *Camelot*
Francis Ford Coppola's *Finian's Rainbow*
and, I think, *The Alamo*
            (the Mission church you can
                        see on the back cover of the album)

Reprise supplied some limber-limbed damzels
who frolicked with us for the session
clad in scantness
                and breasts exposed
                            in the F Troop air

We learned that the Week of April 22
had been designated as "D for Decency Week" in Los Angeles
by the LA County Board of Supervisors

We noted a groovy "Stamp out Smut" poster

We couldn't let that pass by without
                              some fun
We selected a Supervisor named Warren Dorn
for our focus
He had been particularly vehement
                        against erotic literature

We were scheduled to play a
            large psychedelic club, with a rotating stage,

called the Kaleidoscope the weekend of April 26–27

The press release from the Kaleidoscope
was headlined:
FUGS PERFORM MAGIC RITE
FOR WARREN DORN
DURING DECENCY WEEK

".....The Fugs will lead a gathering of gropers, chanters, lovers
and toe freaks in a magic ceremony to be performed in a 1938
Dodge, the back seat of which is an important symbol of the
American sexual revolution.

"In the parking lot of the Kaleidoscope, where they are currently
engaged, the Fugs will declare National Back Seat Boogie Week and
will conduct a magic rite to sensually refreshen and testicularly
juvenate Supervisor Warren Dorn...."

The club had rented a searchlight
            the night of our rite
                    which beamed white tunnels
                            of psychelalic allure
                                    up toward Aquarius

There was an
            anarcho-Bacchic Goof Strut parade
into the parking lot of the club
behind the mint condition '38 Dodge
            (similar to a Kienholz work at the L.A. museum)

A woman volunteer in a green gown
lay supine in the back seat
            holding a carrot
                    waiting to erotomotivate
into the dreams and mind of Mr. Dorn
and ball him

It had a kind of pizzazz
            the visual of the woman
                    in rustling green
                            through the back seat window

as we spread a line of cornmeal around
the Dodge

and just as at the Pentagon and Senator McCarthy's grave
I tried to give the
rite my finest sing-song C chord

chanting such sizzling lines as
        "I exorcise the circle in the name of the Divine Toe"

                    and

    "Arise ! Arise! Eye of Horus! Arise Toe Freaks!
    Arise! Sir Francis Dashwood! Arise Tyrone Power!
    Arise! Arise! Spirits of heaven! Arise William Blake!"

The green gowned deva then
            suck-licked the carrot
                    in oneirophalloerotic mimesis
                    as she was "chant-hainted"
                    into Mr. Dorn's Decency Week dream.

Afterwards I led the crowd
            in a few minutes of "Ommmm"
and then we sang
            "My Country 'Tis of Thee"

before retiring to
            the Tropicana to party.

    I was very tired of exorcisms
    and did no more
            after the carrot-licking
            woman in the green dress.

Meanwhile back in New York
while I was in California
the Yippies were planning their Yip-Out
                        in Central Park
                    on Easter Sunday April 21

Theoretically,
    it should have been a big event
        to put the oomph back into the Festival of Life
            drained by the
                fear from the Yip-In.

Three days before the Yip-out
an 8 page press packet
        was lofted unto the media
including a poster with a headline:
        "YIP-OUT
        RESURRECTION OF FREE
        CENTRAL PARK/ALL DAY/EASTER SUNDAY"

"A be-in is an emotional United Nations"
            the poster read
and on the cover of the packet
a couple fucking, she on top,
        his hands on her ass
on top of an map of America
        with a circle drawn
           around Chicago:

On the inside of the press packet
facing a page that contained an image of Buddha

was the kind of thing
that made the secret police
start clipping Yippie stuff for the files:
instructions on how to make a
whiskey bottle fire bomb

As for the Yip-Out
it had a kind of open-mike quality
& did not make a lasting impression
in neosocialist circles
or in the tracks of time.

April 21–May 1
There was a big nationwide demonstration
organized by Students for a Democratic Society
with rallies, teach-ins, sit-ins, marches

On the 26th a million students boycotted classes

It was overshadowed by events at Columbia U
but the secret police
knew of it,
clip clip snap snap file file.

The Fugs remained a few extra days in Los Angeles
after Decency Week
waiting for some gigs in Portland and Eugene
Five weeks was a long tour
for the hard-partying Fugs
& we missed the beginning of the Columbia take-over

I was feeling tentatively confident
even with Martin King shot
so I put together a tape of thirteen songs
including Allen Ginsberg singing his
setting of Blake's Grey Monk
(which he recited later so stunningly
in Grant Park

                        just before the police attack in Chicago)

For reasons
        I'm not quite able to grasp
                (listening to the tape almost 30 years later)
I thought maybe Joan Baez and others
                might record some of my works
    —one of which was probably the only
        song in the history of rock and roll
                about Samuel Beckett's character Murphy
                    tying himself up
                        in a rocking chair—

            so I had an engineer
                    at Warner Brothers
                        make some copies
                which I mailed here and there
                    in fameland.

Around the time the Fugs were in L.A. that April
            Dennis Wilson
            drummer for the vastly successful Beach Boys
            with their clear perfect harmonies
            and their songs of damozels, beaches, hotrods, surfing
                    & a frozen image of summer
            picked up Patricia Krenwinkel
            & a Garboesque beauty named Yeller
            hitching in Topanga Canyon
            & brought them to his
                    estate at 14440 Sunset Boulevard
            once Will Rogers' place
            with a swimming pool
                        shaped like the State of California

        Wilson
                spent time with them
            and left them there
            to go to a recording session
            and when he returned at 3 AM

there was a school bus painted all black
with the words "Holywood Productions"
on the side

In his living room
was a guy with a guitar named Charles Manson
and about 20 caressing damozels
plus a few guys
followers
living it up
in the twists of no tomorrow

the beginning of a multi-month mooch

The black bus borrowed
many concepts from the
Merry Pranksters, the Diggers,
and the Hog Farm
(such as garbage runs
tons of good food
tossed away in California
They used Wilson's Rolls for garbage runs)

Manson
gave away
the drummer's gold records
and rock king attire
& Wilson called him the Wizard
in interviews.

Manson had studied the guitar during long years in prison
and had a voice that attempted a vowel-path
somewhere between Elvis and Johnny Mathis
but had a kind of watery slosh to it
like too many unknown cans in a hippie soup

He had a fascination with subservience
hungered for a record deal
and hungered for Wilson's fame.

COLUMBIA

The roots of a grab
　　　　are never so simple
but after a long run of events
the take-over at Columbia began on the 23rd
while we were in California

　　　　　　The stodgy, elitist, authoritarian clique
　　　　　　running the university

　　　　　　seemed to rhyme with the kind of thing
　　　　　　　　　　　　　　　　that started wars

At a memorial for Martin King
Columbia president Grayson Kirk
refused to join hands with students
　　　　and sing "We Shall Overcome"

For several years SDS had
　　　　demanded the end of CIA recruiting on campus

The activists had several minds
　　　　　　which formed coalitions of agreement
　　　　　　　　　　　　　on this and that
　　　　　　　　　　　& now and then

　　　　　　By the fall of '67
　　　　　　there was the well-known split in SDS
　　　　　　'tween the action faction & the praxis axis

The university proposed taking
　　　　　　some Harlem land for a gymnasium
　　　　　　　　　　　with separate entrances for
　　　　　　　　　　　students and the "community"

The IDA & its secret defense work
　　　　　　in an era of napalm, assassination plots,
　　　　　　　　　　　& fragmentation bombs

                                                        was an issue

The arbitrary and unilateral decisions
        tinged with authoritarianism
                                of the Columbia adminstration
                                        were issues

but, of course, "The Issue is not the Issue"
                                the famous Berkeley slogan decreed

                And so, on April 23,
                there was a rally
                in front of Grayson Kirk's office
                                to protest the placing of 6 SDS leaders
                                on probation for demonstrations

                which turned into an action
                                at the construction site
                                                of the gym

                A member of SAS (Students' Afro-American Society)
                urged the rally to storm it

                A few hundred quick-walked to the gym
                                tearing down a fence
                                        & blocking some construction equipment
                then marched back to campus

                "Seize Hamilton!" someone shouted
                and then,
                        as natural as natural food
                                they took the hall,
                                the home of Columbia College

                seizing the dean hostage

                During the next three days
                around 1,000 students and activists
                liberated
                five buildings
                including the Low Library office of Grayson Kirk

One day Mathematics Hall
                with its flow of numbers
the next day
        it was packed with SDS and leftists
and renamed LIBERATED ZONE 5

with the red flag of Rev
and the black of Anarchia
                starkly elegant, freshly defiant.
Leftists also grabbed Low

        Tom Hayden (non Columbia student)
        chaired Mathematics— he'd come over from
        Newark where he'd been a housing organizer
        Abbie Hoffman
                stayed there too.

Blacks were in Hamilton
        where they decided to toss out the SDS whitebread
                (There was a long debate
                        on whether to leave)
Hippies and grad students in Fayerweather
Visionary architects in Avery

On campus people wore colors like ancient Byzantium
                Red armbands for strikers
                Blue for jocks and conservatives
                White for faculty
                Green for amnesty supporters

        There were fistfights
        Jocks surrounded Low
        threatening to evict

The Columbia take-over
with its spontaneity, thrill,
                and sense of the forbidden
and those soon in France
gave millions in cadres
                all over the nation

a false sense of standing full square
on the bookcover of Turgenev's *On the Eve.*

Meanwhile, on April 26
the new Sec of Defense
Clark Clifford
informed the press
of a new riot control center
at the Pentagon

honk honk
go the geese of Canada

Saturday April 27
Big antiwar parade down 5th Ave
to the Sheep Meadow
MLK was to have been a speaker
sponsored by the 5th Ave Peace Parade Committee

quack quack
go the ducks of derision

Hair had opened on B'way
& the middle class paid plenty
for nipples & dongs
& singable songs
It was Hippie Capitalism free from
the actual reality
of the Lower East Side police, for instance,
bashing the urban communes &
crash-pads

April 29 the Poor People's Campaign began in DC
without the spirit of its Genius

and then before dawn
on the 30th
the NYPD
brutally removed Columbia protestors
from five buildings they had occupied

                    for several days

The police were worse than at the Yip-In
Strikers were pulled out of buildings
clubbed
          made to run whacking gauntlets
                    and beaten into paddy wagons

     so that of the 712 arrested
     there were 148 with head injuries

and then a general strike began
                    that kept the university closed
                                   for the rest of May

                    President Kirk resigned
                    de facto amnesty was granted
                    the university pulled out of the IDA
     & the gym was never built

but nothing stopped the cannibal napalm
and the era-wrecking
               devoration of the War Caste.

Plus, the right used Columbia
                    to overstate the danger from SDS

as when the right wing business paper called Barron's
warned on its front page:

     "The siege tactics which disrupted Columbia...
       represent the latest attempt by a revolutionary movement
       which aims to seize first the universities and then
                                   the industries of America."

LIBERTÉ ÉGALITÉ FRATERNITÉ

In early May
the ghosts of 1789
danced into Paris
    with those three thrilling words:
    Liberté, Égalité and Fraternité
        as they do every few decades—
for another great
        tossing it up for the Goddess of Grabs.

    Back in March
    there had been attacks
        on U.S. facilities in Paris
      over Vietnam
    Several were arrested from the University
    in the Parisian suburb of Nanterre,
        a subsidiary of the Sorbonne
    Then students
    had taken over the administrative building
        of the faculty

    Though there's no movement in World Civ
    with more splintery factions
        than the French Left
    at that moment, March 22,
    seemingly led by Daniel Cohn-Bendit
    a coalition of Guevarists, Anarchists,
    and Trotskyites
        from the Nanterre faculty
        formed a coalition
            to occupy the college

    This was the movement known as *Le 22 Mars*

    They were driven out of the buildings
    and on May 3
        took refuge at the
    Sorbonne in Paris

It was then the ghosts of '89
did the World is Watching dance of '68

and the well-organized cadres
                    of various factions
went into a rock-throwing,
                    car-burning, poster-pasting,
        barricade-building
war with the bourgeois State.

Throughout the May month
there were riots
and just about every university
                        in the nation
                            was closed.

The smell, touch and sound of it
was caught in a fine piece
by Jean-Jacques Lebel
        published in the U.S. underground papers

    how "the non-stalinist nuances on the extreme left"
    were yearning in desperation
                    for a revolution

The Trotskyist students
            had about 2,000 disciplined members
and were active on the streets
Their paper was REVOLTES
Another Trotskyist faction had
            a paper called AVANT-GARDE

        Lebel judged them
        "the most active, determined and spontaneously
        revolutionary force in the movement. The bourgeois
        and stalinist press picked out one of them,
        Cohn-Bendit, and made him famous by insulting him
        and slandering him."

            Grabs brought forth the
                invisible keys to the nation
                    & tossed them into the sooty air

A million took to the streets
        in a spontaneous swell
"At last the spark has caught the wick,"
                Jean-Jacques wrote

        "Of course, the general feeling is of trance.
        We are high, higher than on a psychovitamin trip,
        high of Great Marriage of our creative subconscious
        poetic energies and of the revolutionary
        collective consciousness,
        high like coming out of the long nothingness
        which was being caught in the fascist structure,
        high of having surpassed our egos at last
        and flowing into a vast electric current,
        high like zombies suddenly turned into human beings
        and saying
                'WE EXIST, WE ARE ALIVE.'"

The radio kept people at barricades informed
        of what's happening

        20,000 students occupied the Latin Quarter

Barge traffic stopped, the ports shut down
No trains   No planes
No mail

It was much much more connected
                with the workers
                        than in the United States.

When workers are well organized
that is, "know the new facts early"
they can respond very quickly
     when industry tries
          to lower conditions
and so in France in '68
farmers on their tractors
   came to the cities, joining students
        demanding: full employment
                   fair taxation
                   higher income
                   larger voice in government

It wasn't just students
and the crisis was sudden
thus revealing
     the power of hidden conflicts
   in back of the pompous masks
          of the Gaullist government

     The government
     managed to build up vast gold reserves
           while spending plenty of money
     and they tried to suck the costs
           out of the workers
     The French know how
        to mobilize
          for instant strikes
            It's one of their glories.

   As a result there was the Grenoble Protocol
   in which French industrialists

had to give 10% wage increases in '68
plus rises in industrial min wage and agricultural min
wage
            & 1-to-2-hour work week reductions

Even though I was
            following France
                    in newspapers
                            from the road

I could feel the thrill of
                    those ghosts of '89

                Liberté Fraternité Égalité

CHANT TO POSTERS

It was a year of marvelous posters
especially in France

This is a chant to all the beautiful protest posters
            made in the haste of going
            made in the church basements
            made in the dorms
            made on the hoods of autos
            made in the union hall

This is a chant to all the beautiful protest posters
            oak tag, markers, paint, glue, brushes
            the brush strokes of ten million posters of '68
            glow in a galaxy somewhere
                            like a glyphic trail

    On May 2
            thirty jets
                    flew over Jerusalem
                            in the shape of a Star of David

with clouds behind them
for Israel's 20th anniversary celebration

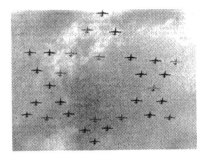

ROBO BY MAY

If we accept the paradigm
of it taking the CIA robo-washers
a few months to program
                    a killer

then Sirhan was likely a robo-killer by May

I think that the intelligence agency robot-makers
had public interfaces,
              probably some hynotists in L.A.
(and maybe a little cult or two)

recruited killers
did background checks
        and did their work on them
                      preparing them to kill

        I have in mind a
        place where
              Sirhan Sirhan
        might have been robo-washed
                            in L.A.

Robowashing, serial murder, napalm,

what a century

but far from the thoughts of the Fugs
when we flew up to Portland May 3
                    after our fun in L.A.
                              for a gig there
          and the next day in Eugene
          the students were occupying the streets of Paris
          just about the time
          we played at a club called the Lemon Tree
                              by a beaver pond

          Before the performance
          I walked out to water's edge
          I had to go back in my mind
          to the lakes of my youth
          to Olson's Belovéd Lake
          to find such a sense of peace
          or Elvis Presley's rendition of
                         "Peace in the Valley"
                              which helped me through
                                   the grief of my mother's death

          The beaver pond
                    by the Lemon Tree
                         was the best time for me in '68

          and I jotted it down for the files:

          "*From an Oregon Tour*

                    (a)
          Do not treat us a loathsome dirt
          o God,

          who have not chosen,
          nor kill us too soon
          before we might have
          touched or seen.

          I will brave
          the twistings of wind,

to meet Thee
above the v-shaped
trail of the beaver
in the stream.

I will hold within
the shriveled core of fear,

that I might find
Thee in the spirits

of the glen
in the first-glazed
ghosts of mist I see adrift awhirl aswirl
upon the dusk-ivory water

in some body-sense of pax
at last
after 28 young years

       (b)

the steam rises above the broken branches
the beaver seen from the window of the nightclub
mixed-log harmony
fills us with longing for the unutterable modes
of the marvelous
before we must climb onto the stage and sing
to the buckskin paisley painted patrons.

It will not be for long
that we will be alone
we are the batter
poured and impuissant."

After that jotting
      I left the mixed-log harmony of
                the beaver dam

and sang, drank, smoked pot & partied.

The Fugs were back in the Lower East Side
                              the 4th of May when
                    Native Dancer's son
                              Dancer's Image
          won the Kentucky Derby
                              by a length and a half
          but then a piss-check
                    while they were wiping it down
          by a Racing Commission chemist
          showed traces of the anti-inflammatory drug
                                        phenylbutazone

          and Dancer's Image was disqualified,
          but later, under appeal,
                    the victory was upheld

          as the surge toward
          the monitoring of fluids
                              continued.

We heard how brutal the police had been
                              at Columbia

Tuli and I went up there
                    to read some poetry
                              and give support to the strikers

just as *Rosemary's Baby* was getting ready to open
                              and the oo-ee-oo of its soundtrack
                                        grew louder and louder

MILLIONS OF HANDS

          Meanwhile, in skillful use of the motorcade
          Robert Kennedy had opened
                              the populist page
          his family so skillfully
                    placed on the iron lectern

          His motorcades

RFK in an open convertible
pulsed from black to brown to ethnic neighborhoods
and always they poured to the sidewalks
black hands, pole hands, irish hands, czech hands

as if on some   dream-time cave wall
reaching for the promise
of America
                    that Kennedy was chanting

Kennedy looked down from his open car
toward dusk
            he could tell the neighborhood had changed
         by the color of the hands outstretched
                    the accents of those that shouted
                              and the names on stores

and then at night
his security team would hide the autos
                    to prevent creeps from wiring bombs

May 6
   the Monday before the Indiana primary
   he motorcaded for 14 hours
   across the south of the state
            At 1:30 am in Indianapolis
                  he went to Sam's Attic
                        with friends
                              and had food
            answered q's
                  his hands red
                        from thousandfold shakings
   till after 3
   and then at 11 am
   RFK played touch football
            on the lawn of the Holiday Inn

   and then in the evening to learn
                  he'd won his first primary!

I liked Robert Kennedy
　　　　I was hungering for his Presidency
　　　　　　　Jack Newfield once told me
RFK frowned at cursing on his staff
I thought,
　　　　"better a liberal puritan
　　　　　　than a dirty-mouthed part-fascist populist"

　　　　　　The Yippies I remember were glum
　　　　　　Kennedy was able to reach out to the people
　　　　　　in ways that war-painted dopesters
　　　　　　　　　　　　　　could not

　　　　　　& the rock stars had run from Yippie
　　　　　　　　　　　　　like bad acid

　　　　　　and so, with dwindling vim,
　　　　　　a plan had evolved for the Yippies to take a few
　　　　　　　　pyschedelic buses
　　　　　　　　tipis and YIP-yurts
　　　　　　　　on a cross-country jaunt to
　　　　　　　　　　　　the Democratic convention

FBI Seeks Depravo Data

Meanwhile, the FBI set up in early May a
a new branch of its Counterintelligence Program
　　　　　　　　　　　　on the New Left

One of the first goals was to smear what they called
　　　　　　　　　　　　Key Activists—
a Bureau Memorandum of 5-9-68 stark-inked it:

　　"The New Left has on many occasions viciously and
scurrilously attacked the Director and the Bureau in an attempt to
hamper our investigation of it and to drive us off the college
campuses. With this in mind, it is our recommendation that a new
Counterintelligence Program be designed to neutralize the New
Left and the Key Activists....
　　"The purpose of this program is to expose, disrupt and

117

otherwise neutralize the activities of this groups and persons
connected with it...."

All FBI offices
were required to "submit an analysis of possible
counterintelligence operations on the New Left and
on the Key Activists on or before 6-1-68."

The secret police
looked in behind the leaflets
& rubbed their
hands in glee
how easy how pleasy
to ruin the left
They got professors fired
They stirred up trouble
with credit agencies
They fired off anonymous
hate-stir letters
by the hostile bushel
They set up faction 'gainst faction
evil for good
and laid down a sneer-song in the time-track

The Fugs went on a tour
of Sweden and Denmark
May 6–13
with the bands Ten Years After
and Fleetwood Mac

Fleetwood, which later filled hockey arenas,
was our opening act

It coincided with all the action in France

Monday May 6   a tour-opening press conference
at Jazz House, Montmartre
in Copenhagen

Tuesday May 7 Two concerts

118

                    Falkoner Centret
                    Copenhagen
Wednesday May 8 Fugs press conference in Gothenberg
and then, that night, a shocking concert
by Bill Haley and the Comets
                    at the big city auditorium.
The crowd chanted,
"Ve want Beill Haley! ve want Beill Haley!"
and we were astounded that Haley was doing almost the
SAME SET! as when I saw him
        at the Municipal Auditorium
                        in Kansas City in 1956
Rudy got up on his standup bass and rode it,
                        just as in '56

Thursday May 9
            Two concerts at Liseberg, Gothenberg
On May 10 we flew to Stockholm
        for a TV show
        a meeting with American draft resisters
        and two performances at Congress Hall

while in Paris the same day
the group known as Le 22 Mars
invaded a class on Nietzsche
        and demanded participation
                    in the General Strike
The faculty
        voted to strike

and the demos took over the Latin Quarter
                        by midnight
a set of days
    in which the police
        rose up to attack
                    the 20,000 rebels at the barricades

The Fugs on the 11th flew up near the Arctic Circle
to Umea to sing at the University

and the12th south to Copenhagen
for two gigs at

the Studenterforeningen

Doing a mudra Ginsberg taught me
Copenhagen, '68

The next day we took the hydrofoil across the harbor
to Lund, Sweden
      two concerts at the University
      and a visit to the famous
            pornographic art show

In France
    On the 13th a day and night of nationwide strike
    by 100s of 1,000s
    and on the 14th students occupy the Sorbonne

            as we boarded the SAS flight
              back to the U.S.

TRYING TO FINISH AN ALBUM

Right away I leaped back into
        a bunch of pot-suffused '60s recording sessions
          with thousandfold tiny adjustments of knobs and faders
            to finish the album
I was making long lists
      of possible titles

It got down to where it was either
Rapture of the Deep
            (Miriam's idea because of our giddy behavior
                              when we were so tired in Sweden)
        or *It Crawled into My Hand, Honest*

It was getting expensive
I didn't like a number of the tunes recorded
                              back in March and April
            Tuli wrote some new ones,
            and so did I,
                  to try to match the
                              best brains on tape

May 17
      Fathers Dan and Philip Berrigan
        John Hogan, Tom Lewis and George Mische
            removed the draft files
                  from a draft board in Catonsville, Md
            and burned them outside
                              with homemade napalm

May 17
      The 9:45 A.M. entry in Sirhan Sirhan's diary
                              on May 18:

"My determination to eliminate R.F.K. is becoming more the
more of an unshakable obsession   port wine   port wine   port
wine R.F.K. must die—RFK must be killed Robert F. Kennedy
must be assassinated R.F.K. must be assassinated R. F. K must
be assassinated R.F.K. must be assassinated..."
      and repeated nine more times before the grim words:

"Robert F. Kennedy must be assassinated before 5 June '68..."

Although it appears to me that the words 5 June '68
                  were written in a different handwriting
and that the pages of this diary
                  might have been written during robo-mumble

Anything mentioned in the presence of a subject
under hypnosis is automatically etched into his mind
especially if it comes from the hypnotist,
and it might flow out at any time

His handlers could have
made sure incriminating notebooks
were written, or perhaps
Mr. Sirhan might have quick-scripted
some of his note pages
in a "trance regression"

On May 20
    There was a benefit for the Black Panthers
                at Bill Graham's Fillmore East on 2nd Avenue
    The reviewer for *RAT Subterranean News*
    walked out in disgust at the
                black is good/white is trash tone of
                                    the perf-flow

On the same day
    millions in France occupied factories, offices, mines

122

and on May 23
            riots began again in Paris

The May–June French strikes
        kept the French economy
                        from heaving
                the usual money
                            to the control class

But, just as in the USA,
            it didn't take too many burnt cars
                for regular folk
                            to have had it with street strife
so that by the end of June
                the Gaullists gained almost 100 seats
                                    in the French Assembly

and of course the riots quelled not the flow of Ploutos
        At the Palais Galliéra
                in Paris
                        someone plunked down $85,000
                                for a Louis IV lacquer commode

                    Flow on!
                    Flow on!

and in New York
        Elizabeth Taylor set a world's record
        for an emerald-cut diamond of 33.19 carats
        $305K
                at Parke-Bernet's

                    Flow, Ploutos, flow!

The valedictorian
            at the Dartmouth graduation
            urged his classmates to dodge the draft
                            and go to Canada

    & the War Caste gritted its teeth

Honk honk
go the geese of Canada

> May 26 Robert Kennedy spoke
> at a synagogue in Portland
> wearing a yarmulke
> & vowing unwavering commitment
> > to Israel

> Kennedy's talk was seen around the nation
> apparently also by Sirhan Sirhan
> > who seems to have left the room
> > with his hands on his ears

> During his run for the Presidency
> the Senator spoke of his doubts
> > about his brother's assassination

> A person close to RFK
> determined that Kennedy was doing his
> own investigation of JFK

> He was bothered by an AP story from Oxnard, Calif
> on 11-23-63:

"A telephone company executive said that 20 minutes before President Kennedy was assassinated a woman caller was overheard whispering:

"'The President is going to be killed.'

"Ray Sheehan, manager of the Oxnard division of general Telephone Company, said the caller 'stumbled into our operator's circuits,' perhaps by misdialing.

"Sheehan said the woman 'seemed to be a little bit disturbed.' Besides predicting the President's death, he said, she 'mumbled several incoherent things.'

"Sheehan said the call was reported to the Federal Bureau of Investigation in Los Angeles but not until after the President had been shot. Until then, he said, it appeared to have been just another crank call.

"Sheehan said there was no way to trace the call. All he could say was that it originated in the Oxnard-Camarillo area some

50 miles north of Los Angeles.

"The FBI in Los Angeles declined to comment.

"Sheehan said one telephone supervisor called another one onto her line after getting the call. He said both supervisors heard the woman say the President would be killed.

"Sheehan said the call was received at 10:10 A.M., Pacific time. The President was shot in Dallas shortly after 10:30 A.M.

"Sheehan said he doesn't think the caller was ever connected with another party. He said she may not have known she had supervisors on the line and may have just been talking to no one in particular."

In late May of '68
    RFK was flying up and down
        for votes in the California and Oregon primaries.

During a stop in Oregon
    Kennedy told a friend that he intended to stop
    off in Oxnard to try to learn anything more about
        the strange phone call•

On May 28
Kennedy did fly into Oxnard
& disappeared for two hours. When he returned he said
he had lost his hat
    and had spent the two hours looking for it.

    He was delayed returning to Oregon
    The official excuse was
        foggy flying conditions

The Oxnard day
    ·vas primary day in Oregon
Kennedy lost to McCarthy 44.7 percent to 38.8

In the hotel in Portland
Kennedy came down
    through the hotel kitchen
        to address his supporters
           in the ballroom

something Sirhan's handlers might well have noted.

By the time Kennedy had given his
                              speech of defeat that night
Sirhan had left
a meeting of the Rosicrucian Society
                        at 2031 East Villa
                                    in Pasadena

May 30
        The Beatles began the White Double Album
                              at the Abbey Road studios in London
        Yoko Ono was on hand for the first time
        as the young men
        did take one through eighteen
                        of "Revolution 1"

        —the last six minutes of the final take
                        were used as "Revolution 9"

Our managers,
        Peter Edmiston & Charles Rothschild•
had booked us into Bill Graham's
                        Fillmore East
                        May 31–June 1
and I decided to record the gigs
                        for a live album

Moby Grape and Gary Burton
                        were on the same bill•

        (The Fugs had performed at Graham's first production,
        a benefit for the S.F. Mime Troupe in the fall of '65
        with the Mothers of Invention and others.
        He'd written a couple of times
                        wanting us to perform
                                    at the Fillmore
        and now it was happening)

I added some musicians to our lineup
so that we were eleven on stage
and laid down the tracks
                for the album called *Golden Filth*

It wasn't our finest
                though fans keep talking about it
                                decades later

I recall how during the intro to one of our tunes
we analyzed Robert Kennedy
                for his putative ruthlessness
one of the Fugs called him
                        an "amphetamine wolverine,"
which I later edited out of the time-flow

WARHOL

A writer named Valerie Solanas
had visited me at Peace Eye
with a 21 page manuscript she asked me to publish
called the *S.C.U.M. Manifesto*

SCUM, of course, was the Society to Cut Up Men
and began
        "Life in this society being, at best, an utter bore
        and no aspect of society being at all relevant
        to women, there remains to civic-minded,
        responsible, thrill-seeking females only to
        overthrow the government, eliminate the money
        system, institute complete automation and
        destroy the male sex."

I'd had it a while
She'd stopped by Peace Eye
a couple of times
wanting to know if I were going to print it
Then she'd left a note
                in late May
she wanted the manuscript back

I got the impression from my staff
                    that she was miffed

Valerie had submitted the S.C.U.M. Manifesto
to Maurice Girodias at Olympia Press
                    and she was miffed at him also

She'd had a part in Andy Warhol's
                    I, A Man
reportedly as a tough lesbian
who turns down a pick-up ploy
                    from a guy in an elevator

She'd submitted a film script
                    a bit too erotic for Andy
and somehow
        building up toward June
                came to believe he was
                        stealing her intellectual property

That spring Warhol had moved his famous "Factory"
a combination salon, in-crowd scrounge lounge,
                and a film/art production studio
from 47th Street to a 4th floor place
                    at 33 Union Square
on the north side of the park.
It was more of a movie set
with two big rooms
                    and a projection booth

Late Monday afternoon, June 3
Valerie Solanas took the elevator to the 4th floor
She'd had come by earlier in the afternoon
                        looking for Mr. W

This time Warhol was there, as were Paul Morrissey,
Fred Hughes, and
        the publisher of an English art magazine, Mario Amaya,

It may have been an error for Mr. Hughes
        to greet the author with
                "You still writing dirty books, Valerie?"

128

The telephone rang
          and Andy was on the phone
          with the writer known as Viva,
          star of *Nude Restaurant*
          and *Chelsea Girls*

Solanas slid a .32 automatic out of her trenchcoat
     and aimed it at Warhol,
     who shouted,
          "Valerie! Don't do it! No! No!"
                         and pinged him

She then chased Mario Amaya and shot him also
Amaya fled bleeding into the other room
                         and held the door
          while Solanas shoved against it
               apparently intent on further pinging
Paul Morrisey sprinted into the projection room
     and watched her through the small window

     The author of the *S.C.U.M. Manifesto*
     next sought to ping the
               young man named Hughes
     who had punched the elevator button
     while she was trying to push open
     the door the wounded Amaya
                    was holding shut

     Hughes dropped to his knees
               and begged of his innocence
     and was still in the beseeching mode
     when the elevator opened
     & Solanas
          fled downward

Someone telephoned Miriam and me on Avenue A that Valerie
had shot Andy

Uh oh, I thought.
I was afraid she might next be visiting
          Peace Eye bookstore,

                    just down the street from our apartment
          to ping me for not publishing her manifesto
          and so I stayed indoors
                    till she turned herself in three hours later
                                                  on Times Square.

Warhol survived
          & Valerie Solanas was sent first to Bellevue
                              then to Elmhurst Hospital
                                             as a bonk bonk

          June 3
          was the final day of the California campaign
          RFK flew L.A. to S.F.
                              for a motorcade
          The streets were 3-deep
          Bobbie and Ethel
                              stood in the back seat.
          In Chinatown
          six loud shots
          Ethel sat down at once
          hunched over
          but RFK stood in place
          waving and smiling
          as the cherry bombs banged

          Then down to a park
                              jammed with 6,000
                                             in Long Beach
          He was very very tired
          Then a motorcade through Watts
          Then to Venice by the beach
          RFK sipping bottle after bottle
                                             of ginger ale
          And a final rally in San Diego
          so tired he had to leave
          to sit head in hands
                              on the stairs from the stage
          before he could return
          to finish his words
                              and hear Andy Williams Sing

June 4
     John Lennon rerecorded the lead vocal
     for "Revolution"
               lying flat on his back
                         at the studio on Abbey Road

That afternoon
     Sirhan Sirhan went target practicing
                    in the company of a pretty young woman
     quick-firing 300 to 400 rounds with a .22
     at the San Gabriel Valley Gun Club
                    in Duarte, not far from his Pasadena home

     the same day Soviet tanks and troops
                    shoved inward into Czechoslovakia
                               ostensibly for maneuvers
     but excuses were found for leaving them•

Robert and Ethel Kennedy
               spent the night in Malibu
                         at the home of John Frankenheimer
     (who'd been making a film of RFK)
Six out of ten of the kids were on hand
The writer Theodore White was there for lunch

In the afternoon
there was a ten mile wind and cold surf
and some went swimming

RFK in trunks
          took 12 yr old David and 3 yr Max
                    to the beach
                         and helped with a sand castle

He saw their son David
          being pulled down by an undertow
                    and swam in and saved him

Then they swam at the house pool
A CBS check of 400 precincts
showed Kennedy leading 49 to 41 o'er McC.

They called K's staff at 3 p.m. with the news

There was a staff meeting in Malibu
on how to patch up things with McC
                      & Humphrey
                      & win over guys like
                      Daley of Chi

      RFK took a nap
      A couple of close RFK aides
      bought themselves bright-hued hippie attire
                 to wear to the victory party
                 that night at a discotheque called The Factory

John Frankenheimer invited
      some hollywood people over
            for an early dinner

Sharon Tate and Roman Polanski
          in the success of *Rosemary's Baby*
                and six others•
RFK was eager to get to his headquarters
          at the Ambassador.

Around then Sirhan Sirhan
      was taking his supper
         at a Bob's Big Boy
           after .22 practice at the gun club

Around 6:30 John Frankenheimer
drove the Kennedys and kids
      with aide Fred Dutton
         in his Rolls Royce Silver Cloud
to the hotel downtown arriving at 7:15

According to an FBI file of an interview with one Peter P. Smith,
an advance man for RFK, who ran his L.A. motorcades,
        the police issued tickets that evening:

"He said that when Senator Kennedy and his party came off
the freeway into L.A. they were met by the police and told that

they could not run any lights. He said that after they proceeded several blocks the crowds began to gather each time the motorcade stopped for a light and that finally the police returned and because they were halting traffic they, the police, took them straight on through the traffic lights to their destination in downtown Los Angeles. He said that then the police issued the motorcade citations for passing the traffic lights."

Kennedy went up to the Royal Suite on the 5th floor
of the 600 room Ambassador
                the same hotel in which the FBI
                        had once bugged Martin King
                                looking for smut

The California polls closed at 8
There was some sort of computer breakdown in L.A.
delaying the count

First CBS predicted victory, then NBC. It was already midnight in the East, and the TV audience was ready for sleep

RFK was both nervous & elated
His son David in blue blazer & grey slacks was by his side,
plus Michael, Courtney, Kerry,
                and a springer spaniel named Freckles

Ethel was wearing an orange and white minidress by Courreges
horizontal stripes above the midriff, large circles below
                        with white stockings

In the Embassy room the crowd was up to maybe 1,800
way above fire code,
                and it was very very warm
The overflow went down one floor
                        to the Ambassador Ballroom

One thing the thousands of pages of FBI files reveal
                was how many film crews
                        from around the world
were positioned in the ballroom

I figure the killers
      had a TV team in the ballroom
            with radio ear piece contact
                  with Sirhan's baby sitters

Sirhan Sirhan had arrived
He'd had a few Tom Collins
Later he couldn't recall
          even under hypnosis
             much of what he did
He went back to his DeSoto
      and brought back his .22
He was seen with a cute young woman
             in a polkadot dress

      About 10:30
      a Western Union teletype operator
      noticed that Sirhan had come over to
      her machine and stood there staring at it
      She asked him what he wanted.
            He didn't answer, just kept staring
      She asked him again
            He just kept staring.
      She said that if he wanted the latest figures on Kennedy
      he'd have to look at the other machine
           He just kept staring.
                RFK Must Die

Outside RFK's door at the hotel
were plenty of reporters
plus a woman with a walky-talky,
             for instance

so that a spotter for the kill-team
          could have easily been there unnoticed

RFK went down one flight to
         speak with NBC
then back up to do the same with CBS,
            then ABC, then Metromedia
He was pitching McCarthy and his supporters
        to join him to deny Humphrey the

nomination

California was the final primary
                and now it was a matter of phone-power,
                                mystique, twisting local Dems
                                                & jostling the War Caste.

Back in his suite
he chatted with Budd Schulberg
                and some of his staff
                                on what to say
He had a gulp of ginger ale
Scanned himself in a mirror
then he was urged to go down

As he left he asked that Al Lowenstein be called
                                (organizer of the '67 Dump Johnson movement)
in New York
to say that RFK'd call him
                                right after the victory speech.

RFK wanted to use the same path downward
                                as back in Oregon

        Very likely his decision
        to use the kitchen path
                        was noted over radios

                        The went down a freight elevator
                        and through the kitchen
                                        into the Embassy Room

        It was a time of playful joy
        He congratulated
        Don Drysdale of the Dodgers
        who'd just won a 3 hit shutout

                        "He pitched his sixth straight shutout tonight
                        and I hope we have as good fortune
                                                in our campaign."

                Hi thanked those who'd helped him

It was very very hot in the ballroom

The pregnent Ethel Kennedy
required security protection
during the speech

on the platform
—the area was shovy-packed,
and one particular cameraman
kept pushing against Ethel—

She complained
(he was situated
right behind her)

"Rosey Grier grabbed him
from behind, placing
one hand around his stomach,
so as to prevent him
from being pushed into Mrs. Kennedy"
                    (FBI KENSAULT interview report)•

The decision
was made by Kennedy's staff
to do a session
            with the pencil press
in the Colonial Room

His security guys were prepared
to take him to the pencils
by side steps off the stage

The winner of California's 178 delegates
congratulated McCarthy
He pointed out that the
"country wants to move in a different direction,
we want to to deal with our own problems
within our country,
            and we want peace in Vietnam."

He was looking forward to "a dialogue, or a debate,"

with Humphrey
"on what direction we want to go in; what we are
going to do in the rural areas of our country, what we
are going to do with those who still suffer
within the United States from hunger...and whether
we're going to continue the policies that have
been so unsuccessful in Vietnam...."

Then he finished,
"We are a great country,
                an unselfish country,
            a compassionate country
        and I intend to make that
        my basis for running....
        so my thanks to all of you
        and now on to Chicago
                        and let's win there."

    The crowd chanted
            in a powerful rhythm
                    "We want Bobby, we want Bobby...."

The orchestra may have been playing
Woody Guthrie's "This Land is Your Land"
                        as the Kennedys made to leave

        His bodyguards
        Olympic hero Rafer Johnson
        and huge LA Rams tackle Rosey Grier
        started to help clear a path to Kennedy's left

        Another tried to lead him to the right
        but a maître d' named Karl Uecker
        parted the gold curtain
                        to the rear
        and led Kennedy
                off the platform's back
        toward the service pantry and the kitchen

        Uecker pulled him along
        toward a deathly right
                        down an incline

and through the double door
                    of the service pantry

It was hasty
"Slow down!" someone cried.
"You're getting ahead of everyone!"

The bodyguards were
                    not yet caught up

On the right was a large
                    floor-to-ceiling icemaking machine
Near it was a low tray stacker

On the left were two stainless steel steam tables
                    that narrowed the passage
                    at one spot to about 6 feet

Sirhan, in a powder blue sports coat
with his .22 stuck into his waist
had been standing on top of the tray stacker
                    with a woman in a polkadot dress
Maybe she was whispering his
                    final wire-up

Now he had gotten down
                    and was waiting
                    in the gloom

There was a sign,
                    THE ONCE AND FUTURE KING
                    on the kitchen wall

    Kennedy stopped by the ice machine
    He was about 30 feet from his destination
                    of a press conference
                    in the Colonial Room

    Then there were shots
    Witnesses gave differing accounts of the number
                    There was an initial quick popping sound

                    then a rapid series
              pop-pop-pop-pop-pop-pop-pop

A named named Thomas Vincent Di Pierro,
              son of a maître d' at the Ambassador
spoke of it to the FBI
                    very soon after
                    in the time of fresh memory:

"I observed a white male and a white female standing on a tray
holder at the opposite end of the ice machine which is
approximately 12–15 feet away. This white male turned toward
the white female and appeared to converse with her very briefly.
He then dismounted from the tray holder [and] went into the
crowd and I did not observe him until shortly thereafter when I
then saw him standing at the heating cabinet behind Mr. Karl
Uecker, another hotel employee. I did not see this white female
again after this time.

"As Senator Kennedy shook the hand of the hotel cook he then
turned to his right in the direction of the heating cabinet and that
time I saw the white male who was previously standing on the tray
cabinet. I saw this individual reach his right arm around Mr.
Uecker and in his hand he had a revolver which was pointed
directly at Senator Kennedy's head...."
                    (Vincent Di Pierro to FBI 6-7-68)•

The woman with whom Sirhan talked on the tray table Di
Pierro described as a white female, 21 to 25, wearing a form-
fitting scoop neck dress. "The dress appeared to have black or
dark violet polka dots."

              A guy named Thane Eugene Cesar
              worked a full day at Lockheed
                            as a maintenance plumber
              and got home (in Simi) to receive a call
              from Ace Guard Service
                            (where he worked part time)
              to go to the Ambassador for guard duty that night.
              Cesar was assigned to escort Kennedy
                            into the Colonial Room
              He apparently grabbed RFK's right arm

with his left
and began pushing back the crowd
in the pantry with his right
before Sirhan fired

Cesar spotted the gun
and saw a red flash from the nozzle
He told the police, "I ducked, because I was as close as Kennedy was.
When I ducked, I threw myself off balance and fell back....
And when I hit...I fell against the iceboxes and the
Senator fell down right in front of me."

Cesar apparently drew his gun
a source of much speculation
by conspiracy buffs
He said he pulled his gun
after the shots
and went to Kennedy's side
"to protect him from further attack."

Dr. Stanley Abo,
summoned from the
crowd,
found RFK
holding his beads & crucifix

"Ethel...Ethel
It's all right
It's ok,"
RFK said,
his body contorting

Pete Hamill looked at his watch:
12:15 AM

Here's What I Believe:
I believe that King and Kennedy
were assassinated
by U.S. Clandestine Intelligence Agencies
probably by the CIA
but I wouldn't put it past a few violent guys

in, say, Naval Intelligence either

& that Sirhan was robowashed
                by secret government experts
and maybe also J. Earl Ray
                in L.A.

That's what I believe
Have believed for a long time

On Avenue A
we had watched the speech
and still had the television lit
when the gun by the icemachine fired

        In Chekhov's story, "Rothschild's Fiddle"
        the dying coffinmaker Yakov
                plays a tune for the Jewish musician Rothschild
        who later performs the melody
        "so passionately sad and full of grief
                        that the listeners weep"

        All that night
        the strings of Rothschild's fiddle
                        trembled my soul
        It was the kind of night
                that made one want to join
                                an intentional community.

Drear morn droned drear
                on a destiny day
I awakened in a pit of ashes
                forlorn and bereft
                        out of sorts with America
                                & wanting a different life
when Jerry Rubin called around noon.
                "Did you hear the good news?" he asked.
"What good news are you talking about?" I replied.

"About Bobbie. Now we can go to Chicago!"

I let what he said
pass by in silence
though I felt more alienated
than someone crawling
in a Beckett novel

Jerry Rubin probably wasn't the only one
exulting over RFK.
Although there are no smoking stockings, of course,
I picture J. Edgar Hoover
rewarding himself with a little lipstick
some rouge, a wig perhaps,
pulling his garter belt
upon his fresh shaved legs
& maybe clicking around his room
in spike heels
to some records
he'd gotten as gifts
at an o.c. casino

June 8
The robo-hobo James Earl Ray
was arrested by Scotland Yard at Heathrow in London

June 10, 11, 12, 13, 20-22
The *obla-di obla-da* factor
suffused the sorrow
and wiped into the grief for RFK
in the convolutions of an art project
just as the plans for the Pentagon Exorcism
had ebbed the grief for Groovy
the preceding fall•
or touring did for Memphis

so that less than a week after RFK
the Fugs began 7
long and exhausting days recording
at Richard Alderson's Impact Sound
on *It Crawled into My Hand, Honest*

I wanted the second side of the record
          to be like a long collage

I was working with the composer Burton Green
on a long piece, with words, called *Beautyway*
                named after a Navaho ceremonial
                            and we had recorded it
but it was not to wind up on the album.
Things were getting expensive: *It Crawled Into My Hand, Honest*
          would wind up costing about $25,000

I abandoned the long, complicated "Magic Rite"
                that we had recorded early in the year
                          because I was getting
              disgusted with the fake short-cuts
                            which substituted
                                  for real change
              (I finally used a short snippet of it on the record—
              the "Irene (Peace)" section at the end of side two)

And I gave up also a tune called
              "The Vision of William Blake's Garden"
              (a version of which can be heard on our CD
              Fugs Live From the Sixties,
              from our spring '69 concert at Rice University)
Now, thirty years later. I sorely wish we'd finished
"William Blake's Garden"
We'd planned to use Olson's mantram
"Act in Creation/Arouse the Nation
Blood is the food of those gone Mad!"
                          as a chanted preamble

              The year had such a frantic pace
              I had to abandoned a number of projects
                                especially in publishing
              Janis kept me apprised of the various famous men
              she'd been balling
              and it helped inspire a publication
                          called "Greta Garbo's Mouth"
                    which was to feature salacious gossip

from the world of rock and roll
                   & the counterculture

In my notebooks are various scandalous
          entries
          such as her comment to me
          after making it with Jim Morrison

This was to be the cover of the first
issue of Greta Garbo's Mouth

POT BUSTS AS POLITICS

Pot busts have often been a government tool
                   to twist the lives of activists

On June 13
narcotics officers showed up at the pad of
               Jerry Rubin and Nancy Kurshan
They said they were investigating a murder in the Bronx
They shoved in
They had no warrant
They roughed him up
They tore up his poster of Fidel
             and called him a Commie
They took him down to the Tombs
                 for possession of bu

To me it looked like another
            instance of grass laws being used
                        against the counterculture

    I didn't like it
    I'd resented it when the Feds tried
            to set up Allen Ginsberg for a pot bust back in '65
    and so at Peace Eye the next day
            I mimeo'd a leaflet
                    and had it distributed
            around Tompkins Park and
                        over by Gem Spa on 2nd Avenue:

        "Last night Jerry Rubin's apartment was invaded by
detectives who were more interested in politics than pot. He was
busted on a felony rap because he allegedly had more than a
quarter of an ounce. The cops made a point of checking
telephone directories, files of letters and ripping up posters of Che
and Fidel. The cops were eager for any information regarding the
Yippies, Chicago, and ESSO (The East Side Service Organization,
a help-the-hippies umbrella group that had gotten money from
the city). Jerry was repeatedly beaten although no charge of
resisting arrest was lodged. Jerry required medical treatment and
had a broken coccyx bone in addition to other injuries. The
androids repeatedly called him a Communist. His apartment is in
total shambles. Bail was $1,000 with no cash alternative because
the Legal Aid lawyer told him he had tried to wreck Columbia and
he wouldn't help him. Bail was raised by all-night canvassing."

            William Kunstler defended him
        "This is clearly a political arrest," said Kunstler,
    "and an attempt to stifle the Yippie demonstrations in Chicago
                    this summer."

Government pressure
            weighed against psychedelia
            against guys like Ken Kesey
                        and Timothy Leary
                            and forced them to change their rap

            just as it did against Blake
            or an ancient Egyptian stonemason

                    wanting to experiment with
                              changes in glyphs

June 19
          50,000 took part in a Solidarity Day March in D.C.
                    to end the Poor People's Campaign

          It showed how much things had changed
                              with the death of King
          for King had vowed
                    that the campaign would continue
                              growing and growing
          till the government actually did something about
                              "jobs, income and a decent life"

          Hoover and the CIA no doubt were happy
                    that Zorro was under the sod
                              and all this talk about the poor
                                        there with him
                              in the dark farm of Dis.

          The same day as the big march
                    Marge Piercy read her poetry
                              as part of the series, "SDS on WBAI, 99.5 FM"

June saw
          Lee Trevino win the U.S. open

          & Stan Freberg's TV commericial for Jeno's frozen pizza,
          starring the Lone Ranger and Tonto,
                    pick up awards at the
                    American Television and Radio Commercials Festival

The Law Commune

A kid named Jerry Lefcourt graduated from NYU same year
                    as I did, '64
then made it through Brooklyn Law in '67

and went to work for Legal Aid
in '68 he organized a group of attorneys
in Legal Aid to protest working conditions
                    and was fired in July
He sued Legal Aid that his free speech was violated
                    He was rep'd by William Kunstler
                    lost case then appealed

His sister-in-law, Carol Hoffman Lefcourt
graduated from Brooklyn Law in '68
She too was hungry to go to the roots
and joined with Jerry & some other young lawyers
in the coming months
                    to found the New York Law Commune
(Later she wrote some important child-support legislation for NY State)

The Commune accepted as given the need
            for fundamental change—
                    It took on radical and civil rights cases

and helped win the famous Panther 21 case in NYC
Two of its members later founded one of the first
                            all-women law firms
Jerry Lefcourt defended Abbie Hoffman in Chicago
                    in the "FUCK"-on-forehead case
and after he was arrested wearing an American flag shirt
                            at a HUAC hearing

The law commune of Lefcourt, Garfinkle, Crain, Cohen,
            Sandler, Lefcourt, Kraft and Stolar:
a bright bright sequence
            in the time-track
        before it dissolved in the Heraclitean panflow•

DIGGERS GRRR-ING AT YIPPIES—
& MAYOR DALEY SHAKING HIS FIST

Everybody in the do-good Counterculture
                    borrowed from the Diggers
The Fugs performed at a Digger
                    outdoor concert in Golden Gate Park

147

in the Spring of Love
The Diggers and the Fugs were both on
                    the same flat bed truck
                        exorcising the Pentagon

By mid-summer '68
there was a split 'tween the Diggers
                        and Yippies
        I'd meet Emmet Grogan on the streets
                    and he'd complain about Rubin & Hoffman

Somewhere about now in the time-track
the ghastly word "media-freak"
            came into parlance

            I think Emmett felt that
                    that's what they were
            particularly Hoffman
            whom he accused
            of stealing Digger tactics
                        for a non-Digger agenda

Grogan, of course, had his imperfections
He'd said some amateurish
                    and homophobic things
at an SDS convention earlier in the year
            (standing up on a table and
            shouting, "Faggots! Fags!"
            as a preamble to a speech, for instance)

As Chicago grew near
Emmet Grogan and another Digger
                    with some volunteers
used Albert Grossman's rock management office
                        on East 56

        to make calls and
                    work the media
        to get kids not to go to Chicago
                for the Rubin/Hoffman follies

Meanwhile, in Chicago Mayor Daley
            ran things

like an understudy to Orson Welles
in a play about a
flawed authoritarian populist
ill-at-ease in epaulets
in a smoke-filled dressing room

In Daley
the puppet and the puppeteer had mutual strings—
I've thought for many years
his arms jerked jively that summer
from the strings of the secret police

No one knew for sure
if Daley had stolen the state for JFK in '60
but that he MIGHT HAVE
gave him a fist
to shake above the city

He lived in a modest house
and did not have a hunger for money
Plus he had the fierce paradigm
of what the tired, angry afterwork American tubestarer
really wanted
clearly in focus.

The underground paper *The Chicago Seed*
proposed a sit-down
'tween city and local Yippies
"to avoid bloodshed and needless hardship"
After that
Daley began harassing the *Seed*
arresting street vendors, for instance
and making things hot

SUMMER ON A

That summer I divided my time
in the slices of too many commitments
'tween our pad on Avenue A
running the Peace Eye Bookstore
recording the record
working on Chicago

and hanging out in the
many bars of the counterculture:
Rafiki's and PeeWee's on Avenue A
& Stanley's, the Annex, and Mazur's on Avenue B,
          plus Slugs, the Old Reliable
                    The Cedar, & many West Village places
                              (such as the Lion's Head)

What a toke of ruination for the liver!
Dr. Nemhauser of Tompkins Square North
          told me to stop drinking
                    that my liver was enlarging

I knew that sometimes it felt outlined
                    like a minimalist neon sculpture.

A few times I helped soldiers fleeing the war
They arrived in their uniforms
and slept in the back room at Peace Eye
They changed into civvies
& the next day
          I tossed away their uniforms
                    here and there
                              in the garbage cans of 10th and 12th

At Peace Eye I printed hundreds of leaflets and fliers
free, including many for the Motherfuckers,
                    even though they'd been mean to me

I strolled around the scene
                    in my red boots or my white boots
attired in necklaces, striped pants
                    Tom Jones shirts and lacey finery
that helped rinse away
          what Kenneth Rexroth once called
                    "The light from Plymouth Rock"

Miriam and Didi went just about every day
to the playgrounds at Tompkins Square Park
Didi had a little bell
          from the Psychedelicatessen
                    she sometimes wore around her wrist

The park was where all the races, cultures and factions
came together
         There was very little open strife

and the streets were safe enough
       that Miriam and Deirdre could go out at 3 AM
           to the Three Guys from Brooklyn vegetable store
                    on First Avenue.

YEAR OF FEAR

It was a time of whispery 'Noia
Part of it was caused by the cosmic
            revelations of acid and psychedelics
which for some was an exhausting perturbation of
Flashbacks Flashforwards & Flashsideways

The old adage "keep a stiff upper lip"
      was translated on Avenue A to
           "keep a calm hallucination"

But that was only a part of the
           Year of Fear
The revelations about the CIA
The suspicion they'd killed JFK
The fact that
      when my mother-in-law called
          she could hear everything in the room
gave a kind of creepy substance to the dread

No one wanted to be fingered a 'noid
And the secret police didn't mind
        if you thought they were everywhere

It was in this context of 'noia
that the novelist H.L. Humes
      universally known as Doc
began to hang out at the Peace Eye Bookstore
Doc and I had been friends
        since 1962
It was through him I first met Harry Smith

who produced the first Fugs album

Doc had been one of the founders of *The Paris Review*
He'd had a huge—something like 755 page—novel
                published called *The Underground City*

Doc had the NOIA.
He thought there was a huge and benevolent
network of computer scientists
who ran a network
                called FIDO

He would stand in Peace Eye up against the bookcases and
talk in a low voice
                sure that FIDO's satellite-based monitoring
                equipment was picking up his words

He also thought the CIA was spreading lowgrade infections
                                in the counterculture
He told me he thought a friend of his
                was a CIA officer
                        who had tried to strangle Sirhan Sirhan
in the kitchen after Kennedy was shot

I helped him get a little rent-controlled pad
                from my landlord Sam Scime
                        on 9th near A

He was very magnetic
                and people would come
into Peace Eye
                to hear him speak

Of course the CIA was paranoid also
                James Angleton, whose counterintelligence section
                        ran the counterculture-killing
                                CHAOS program
                was a noidy-noidy among noidy-noidies.

I felt it also,
        felt myself afraid,

afraid O Lord, afraid
of the Secret Police

I was afraid to talk in public about Cuba
because of the threat from
CIA-funded right wing Cubans
I was afraid, afraid O Lord, afraid
of the Secret Police

Keen for disgrace
Keen for smut
The Secret Police in
Their coffee-cup hut.

At the State University at Stonybrook
(where we'd done the dawn concert early in the year)
there was the World Poetry Conference
June 21–23

and I was invited. Some of my friends,
including Anselm Hollo and George Kimball were there,
as were Donald Hall, Louis Simpson,
Allen Ginsberg, Nicanor Parra,
Zbigniew Hebert, Eugene Guillevec
and many others

There was a party on Saturday, the 22nd
at Louis Simpson's house
in Bell Terre

It was a thronging, well done event
both indoors and out
Donald Hall, that brilliant poet,
was very drunk
and in fact was about to pass out
I myself had drunk so much
my liver was feeling like a
Rudi Stern neon
I overheard a discussion between

a male professor and the wife of another professor
He taunted her,
          "You're nothing without your husband."
I laughed at him,
     and then began to taunt him
                    that he was a nothing also
(After all, Tuli Kupferberg's "Nothing" had
               become one of the Fugs' most popular tunes)
A poet pal
     (now a famous sports reporter)
          came up from behind and
               broke a bottle of champagne over his head.

The result was a broken glass-topped table
                              on the outside patio.

It was then,
     noticing the zzz-zoned Mr. Hall,
we hatched a scheme to say that it was Hall,
a good friend of Louis Simpson,
who had broken the table.

It was years before the gentle bard
          found out it wasn't he who had
                    bacchus'd the broad sheet of glass

During the World Poetry Conference
a number of us stayed in the dorms.
I recall
     Anselm Hollo,
               trying to hurl a typewriter out a window,
but the glass was too tough
whereupon he tossed it down some stairs,
                    a piece of typed-on paper
                              around the roller.

It was a battered relic I couldn't resist retrieving
I kept it for many years
               and wish I still had it.

It was as if America had been in
                    a huge car crash
& we all wanted it to be "normal"

"normal" struggles against the war and racism
normal struggles for a better economy
normal cycles of work and fun
a normal revolution

But, at the Stony Brook World Poetry Conference
I had not yet recovered from MLK, RFK
                    Daley's "Shoot to Kill,"
my own racy time-track &
the strange proclivities of my
                    brothers and sisters at the barricades

No normal, no healing
                    and Olson's line
                    "Blood is the food of those gone mad"
                    was dripping its whispers in my
                                        bacchic noggin

July 1
    62 nations, including US, UK and USSR, signed the nuclear
                                        nonproliferation treaty

FBI MEMO ON TECHNIQUES TO DISRUPT
THE NEW LEFT

Meanwhile, an FBI Memo of
        July 3, 1968
            analyzed the suggestions from FBI offices
                        on disrupting the New Left:

• taking advantage of personal conflicts among New Left leaders
• the creating of impressions that certain
                    New Left leaders are informers
• using underground newspaper articles to
            show "depravity of New Left leaders and members"
• exploiting hostility between New Left groups and orgs such as the
    Progressive Labor Party, which the FBI described as

"a pro-Chinese, Marxist group"
• The use of ridicule, ahh ridicule, against the New Left
• pointing out dope use by New Left
(Memo, Cointelpro head C.D. Brennan
to W.C. Sullivan, at headq'ters)

July 3
    The Beatles began work
                on the theme song of '68
                        "Ob-la-di Ob-la-da"

On July 4 Paul McCartney
                laid down the lead vocals
        in the amazingly fast way
                        their Muses allowed

        Ob-la-di Ob-la-da the war went on
        On skyrocket day in the U.S.
        the Pentagon announced that US combat deaths
                the first six months of '68 exceeded all of 1967

July 7
    I'd written a "persona" song
    called "Johnny Pissoff Meets the Red Angel"
                        after Kennedy's assassination

    I wanted to explore
                the American mean streak
    my own included
    such as when I have Mr. Pissoff sing,
            "I'd love to get my hands on Sirhan Sirhan
            I tear out his spine and shove it down his throat...."

    It was a year when the Imago Violentiae
                    was like an attacking spiral galaxy
                            upon the Imago Mundi.

    I took a bus to Stroudsburg, Pa
            to meet with singer/composer Bob Dorough

whose pleasing Buttermilk Skies tenor
        reminded me of Hoagy Carmichael's
Dorough arranged "Johnny Pissoff," and one
of Tuli's tunes, "Life is Strange,"
            plus a satire on Medieval chants
                called "Marijuana"

In July
    Janis Joplin and Big Brother's *Cheap Thrills*
    went to the stores
            through the Columbia Records flow
    and "went gold" as they say
                with flowing ease

    Robert Crumb did the cover
            for $600
    and was bitter he never received back the original art
    especially when, in the early '90s,
            someone sold it for $20,000
                at an auction at Sotheby's

    The Band's *Music from Big Pink*
    & The Doors' *Waiting for the Sun*
                hit the turntables in July

    and sixteen heart transplant surgeons
                met in Cape Town, South Africa
        the majority of which agreed
            that a blood globulin, ALD (antilymphocyte globulin)
        should be given future heart transplants
            to suppress lymphocytes—
                those white blood cells
                    that destroy foreign tissue

    The LeMans 24 hour sportscar race had been postponed
            for the French strikes
                but was held in July

    the winning car had a 4.9 litre Ford V-8 engine
            which drove 2,765 miles in the 24

CUBAN TERROR

Meanwhile in early July right wing Cubans
began a campaign of bombing and terror

They bombed the Canadian and Australian tourist offices
in NYC on July 5
& July 8
      another bomb hurting two at the NYC Japanese tourist
            (the goal was to stop them
                    from letting travelers
                         go to Cuba)

For decades
    all my adult life
        no real colloquy on Castro and Cuban
could be conducted safely in the United States
because of the threats of right wing Cubans
like a curse of CIA-funded metalwinged
                hornets

In part empowered by right wing drool-heads
in the CIA
the far right Cubans
        successfully prevented
              any full discussion
                in America
                    on the issue of Cuba

The rightite Cubans
        killed liberals within their community
          It was ghastly, evil
              and successful

July 10
    the exiles made
    explosions at the Yugoslav and Cuban missions to the UN

    and on the 13th

they invaded WBNX in NYC
to broadcast anti-Castro statements

July 15
Black Panther co-founder Huey Newton
on trial in Oakland
for killing a policeman
back in October '67

2,500 chanting BP's surrounding Alameda County Courthouse
Newton found guilty
and given 2–15

Meanwhile, the Yippies submitted
a new proposal to Mayor Daley
for the use of Lincoln Park for a 5-day Festival of Life
and for a concluding gathering at Soldiers Field
on August 30
after which everyone would leave Chicago

Daley stalled. Attorney General Ramsey Clark
sent an aide, Roger Wilkins, to meet with the mayor
to ask him to issue permits
to no avail. •

July 17 the Beatles
attended the world premiere
of *Yellow Submarine*
in Piccadilly Circus

The next day they recorded "Helter Skelter"

July 18
the Yugoslav communist Party declared
"unconditional support"
for Czech liberalization
(and Pres Tito
visited Czechoslovakia three weeks later)

July 19
    John Lennon's tune "Maharishi"
            was changed to "Sexie Sadie"
            and recorded on July 19
                        in London

July 21
        the right wing Cubans
        bebombed the Jefferson Book Shop at 100 E. 16th

            and then early in the AM
            on the 26th

            one of them stood with a grenade launcher
            on 80 University Place
                        near the Cedar Bar
            and fired a grenade up into the big
            second story window of Grove Press

            The current issue of the *Evergreen Review*
            —shudder shudder—
            had published sections of Che Guevara's diary

        (A few years later the *New York Daily News* wrote that
        it had been told by a former NYC police commissioner
        that CIA had provided bombs to anti-Castro groups in
        in New York, to be used against leftists.)

            The CIA as of '75 had refused to release
            the contents of 25 files on Grove Press.

            though Army Intelligence had released doc's
            that the Army had intercepted Grove Press' mail.

Also in July
        the ghosts of needles were in the air
        as the poet we all called Szabo
        whom I'd published a number of times
                    in *Fuck You/ A Magazine of the Arts*
        came out of hospital after a long stay
                    with needle hepatitis

160

which ten years later
killed him with liver cancer

July 25–27
The Fugs went back to the Psychedelic Supermarket in Boston
to sing and party
as best the Chicago summer allowed

July 29
Beatles began recording "Hey Jude"
with its long long fade
that limned the decade

The next day there were
huge demonstrations in Mexico City
students and protestors
bashed by Federal troops and police

Students barricaded themselves
in buildings at National University
after excessive force
was used by the police
during minor protests

August 1
The good aspect of Johnson signed a housing bill calling for
$5.3 billion for 1.7 million low cost housing units

In early August
I was desperate to finish *It Crawled into My Hand, Honest*
before the Chicago convention
(where I thought I might be jailed, or worse)
and before our upcoming European tour
I also was designing
the actual layout for the liner notes

We went to Cleveland
to play Le Cave

                    a club where Linda Ronstadt
                    and the Stone Ponies had once performed
We were there from July 30 to August 1
During the daylight I would fly back to New York
                    to mix the album at Alderson's studio
then fly back to the gig

        On Wednesday I went to Ivanhoe drafting supplies
        to get a drafting board
                    which I carried back to NY on the plane
                    to cut and paste
                    the inner fold-out sleeve
                    of *It Crawled into My Hand, Honest*

The bard d.a. levy
            came to one of the gigs
I tried to interest him in coming to Chicago
(He was one I'd asked to send a mantra
                    to chant in the streets)
He'd been publishing the *Buddhist Third Class Junkmail Oracle*
a mix of his brilliant collages, his poems
and the usual look of a tabloid underground paper

He'd just printed his August issue
        in which he announced he was giving it up
                    because of no financial support from the community

He was glum
earlier in the year he'd faced a five year sentence
for reading "obscene" poetry
                    to some teenagers
            in a coffee house in the basement of a cathedral
                                    in Cleveland
and so he had pled *nolo contendere,*
                    though he hated it.

It was the last time I saw him.

        A bunch of bikers had commandeered
                    the stageside tables
                                by threatening the longhairs
                                            in the seats.

162

We often broke things during
                our song "Nothing"
(It was just about our only lighting cue—
                darkness at the end of *Nada*)
and in honor of the chaos of '68
                and in front of d.a. and the bickery bikers
I tore up my beautiful black velvet coat
        with brocaded cuffs
                (in which I had made the mudras
                                in Copenhagen)
                and tossed rough pieces of black
                                out to the Goddess of Grabs

From Cleveland on August 2–3
we flew from Cleveland to Chicago
for a booking at the Electric Circus
                4812 North Clark Street

We stayed
        at the Heart of America Motel
                where we partied in lieu
                                of worrying about Chicago

        I recall the throbbing lights
                and colors in dishes
                                picked up by projectors

        An audience
                some stoned
                        some ready to stone
                        as tie-dyes and gowny grace
                        gave way to teargas and mace.

Then back to N.Y.
        to work around the clock on the album.

To Orientalia, then at 11 East 12
                a beautiful book store
                        I'd been visiting
                since first coming to NY from Mo. in '58

I went on Hiroshima day
   and bought some books
      to chink my leaking Book Boat:

       Iversen SOME ANCIENT EGYP. PAINTS & PIGMENTS
       Hopkins THE COPTIC VERB
       Reiner LINGUISTIC ANALYSIS OF AKKADIAN
       Plototzki STUDIES IN EGYPTIAN & LINGUISTICS
       Idris Shah ORIENTAL MAGIC

I was also looking for power glyphs
            for the album design.

I took a few minutes to
study my old Linear B textbook
          from N.Y.U.
to figure out the Mycenean glyphs for motherfucker:

from my '68 notebook

On August 7
a bunch of us (myself, Richard Goldstein, Krassner, Abbie, Jerry)
flew to Chicago for a meeting.
      with Al Bougher and David Stahl of Daley's office

   It was scorching hot.
   They didn't dig Abbie smoking pot in
          the mayor's office
   We continued to beg for permits
   (but all they would ultimately give us
         was access to one electrical socket
           for one afternoon show
             in Lincoln Park)

The staff at the *Chicago Seed* and Chicago Yippies
wanted the New Yorkers to cancel
activities in Chicago

August was the month
the Lennon tune "Revolution"
came onto the radio playlists
and the marvelous threnody "Hey Jude"
with its famous long fade
& Tom Wolfe's *THE ELECTRIC KOOL-AID ACID TEST*
was published by Farrar Straus
& the Fugs finally finished *It Crawled into My Hand, Honest*

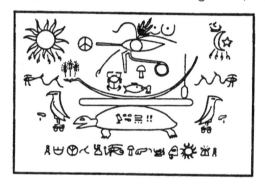

A Glyph from the Liner Notes

In Miami Beach
Tricky won on the first ballot
with Spiro Agnew his running mate.

About the time that Tricky
was beginning to trick,
at a make believe western town
called the Spahn Ranch
used as a grade b movie set
and for Marlboro commercials
on the northern edge of the San Fernando Valley
in a place called Chatsworth
arrived Charles Manson and his family

in their psychedelic bus
They'd been tossed from the Will Rogers/Dennis Wilson mansion

The Spahn Movie Ranch was
just a couple of gallons of gas away
                    from the rich haunts of Hollywood

He asked if he could stay in the Outlaw Shacks
small movable huts looking
                    like damaged motel units from the 1920s

Charlie approached the 80-year-old nearly blind Mr. Spahn
to be allowed to move onto the Western Set itself
where they lived for a while in the jail

Sleazy awnings held up by crooked posts
ran the length of the mockup cowboy main drag boardwalk
There was a fake Rock City Cafe
a jailhouse with wooden-barred cell
the Long Horn Saloon with mirrors, roomlength bar and juke box
a carriage house with old carriages
& an undertaker's parlor

The M group made themselves useful
Several young females made themselves
                    caressingly handy to Spahn
Others fed the horses, and helped rent them out
                                        to tourists

By day it was fantasyland
by night it was acidland
            and a place of communal meals
            singing
                    and many many fornications
by twos, threes, and tens.

There the group
            could further plot
                    the rise of Mr. M
                    as a rock star/therapist-crooner
                                with a Jesus-Satan complex
and a Porsche-stripping stolen car ring on the side.

On the 11th another tragedy
　　my friend Don McNeill
　　　　drowned swimming alone in Lake Mombasha
　　　　　　near his summer cottage
　　　　　　　　　in Orange County upstate

　　　I felt another edgeless desolation
　　　as we sat, a few of us,
　　　in St. Mark's Church
　　　　　　for his memorial service
　　　I remembered
　　　　　his work at Peace Eye
　　　his leather jacket
　　　　　　his search
　　　　　　　　for the perfect commune

The *Voice* published my elegy
　　　　　　"For Don"
　　　　　　　　Here are some of the lines:

　　　"I kiss your tender hand fair brother
　　　I cry for you, for us,
　　　when the lines shift to fill
　　　the bright gap at the barricades"

　　　　　　and

　　　"Anubis guard this man
　　　Khepri lift him up as a beacon in the prow
　　　Jesus share with him the crowned heart of god
　　　Thoth play into his brain the Image of the Earth
　　　and Magna Mater, Woman of the Lake of Thrills
　　　take this man to fulfillment
　　　If you are, and if the sky is lit up with flares,

　　　& Don McNeill, as we move onward
　　　and the old fires fade
　　　receive this for all time
　　　a kiss from your brother's lips"

You can find his single book, *Moving Through Here*,
　　　　　　　　　　in the libraries.

Allen Ginsberg was in San Francisco
Abbie called him and said that city hall was stalling
                    and would Allen stop over in Chicago
                              on his way back to New York

He agreed, and met with deputy mayor Stahl
                              on August 13
          The meeting lasted several hours
               "I asked them to please give a permit
                              to avoid violence"
                    Ginsberg said
                         at the Chicago Seven trial later on.
          He sang "Hare Krishna" for them
                    as an example of the sort of music
                              the Festival promised

          but even Krishna
                    could not shake loose some assembly permits
                              from the ill-willed mayor

Meanwhile
          the haemonara of pizza street
continued to boil the week of August 14
when the Army gave
               riot control training to
                    6,000 combat soldiers in Ft. Hood, Tex

August 15, the Fugs gave their annual free concert
in Tompkins Square Park
     There were so many people
               the park was totally filled
                    and also the surrounding sidewalks

     I'd written a satire against the group called the
     Motherfuckers, whose member had accused
                    me of having a Swiss account
     so we stood like a bunch of Laurence Oliviers
     in *The Entertainer*
     in square topped straw hats and canes
               dancing across the stage crooning
               "Up Against the Wall...."

168

August 16
    Valerie Solanas was declared insane
                    and sent to Mattewan State Hospital

The same day the Fugs flew back to California
                    for some warm-up gigs before Chicago
The cab from LAX to the Tropicana
                    in those days cost $7.30

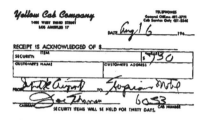

The Fugs played Friday and Saturday, the 15th and 16th,
    at a place The Bank in nearby
                    Torrance, California

It was one of the few times I performed barefoot
            continuing my experiments
                        on rinsing my puritan heritage
    by being the first performer on Warner/Reprise
            to dance barefoot during "Kill for Peace"
                        wearing goldflecked toenail polish

The Cheetah was in financial trouble
                  so, like fools, we did a benefit for
them the Sunday before our weekend gigs there.

The rationale was that they would pay our $4,000
                                 fee out of the benefit

It didn't work,
            and we were burned
                        even though one of the owners
                        of the place was quite wealthy.

Just before midnight, August 20,
Soviet troops, with help from Poland, Hungary,
East Germany and Bulgaria—
            forced themselves into the country—
The 170,000 person Czech army did not fight
but there was resistance
                thousands demonstrating
                        a few tanks burned

Some sat down on the road
                    facing the oncoming tanks

I didn't like it
        The Fugs talked about
                trying to sneak into Czechoslovakia
                        when we were in Europe
                                next month

PROLEGOMENON

        In Early August
            the Yippies published a
                neatly-designed 30 page manual
            for living free in New York City
                called *Fuck the System*

They printed 10,000 copies
I was not involved
It appears to have been
written by Abbie and his friends

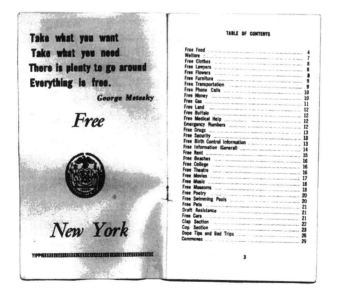

Take what you want
Take what you need
There is plenty to go around
Everything is free.

George Metesky

Free

New York

The text was accurate
                and fairly well written
        such as, say, the section on communes
                which began, "Communes can be a cheap and
enjoyable way to live. They are a good tribal way to live in the
city. Because they are tribes each has a personality of its own.
This personality depends on the people in the commune and how
well they get along together. For this reason the most important
part of setting up a commune is choosing people who are com-
patible. It is vital that no member of the commune has any strong
objection to any other member. More communes have been
destroyed by incompatibility than any other single reason. People
of similar interests (speed freaks with speed freaks, painters with
painters, and revolutionaries with revolutionaries) should get
together."

                On August 18 the *New York Daily News*
                ran a piece on it
                under the headline
                        "New York on $0.00 a Day"
                        and printed the Yippie post office box
                which triggered a
                                big flow of letters
                                        wanting copies.

                Around that time
                        other Yippie items were printed
                such as the official Yippie symbolic
                                        matchbook:

Meanwhile, it didn't look good in Chicago:
No bands
No money
No chance for fun

No place for the fabled quarter of a million
                                to ball by the lake

              Just Yippie shine-ons
              setting some freakly fires
                       in the lens of Mayor Daley's mind—
              But they were frail frail excuses
              for the massive schemes of CIA-CHAOS, FBI Cointelpro
              the NSA, and military intelligence

GARDEN PLOT

          Beginning in '67 the Army Security Agency
                   an arm of the NSA
                   was doing electronic snooping
                   against anti-war people
                                as part of a project called Garden Plot

          In August '68
          the ASA was activated under Garden Plot
          to work in Chicago
          This op was coded "Rancher III"
                   involving the 5th Army in Illinois
                   and units of ASA from III Army Corps in Texas,

          plus ASA and USAFSS units from Warrenton and Arlington, Va.

              The directive ordered ASA, wearing civvies, to
          "provide covert and overt monitoring of Citizen Band and emergency
          nets through the employment of fixed and mobile intercept and
          communications positions."

A writer named Jack Mabley wrote some columns
                                in the *Chicago American*
              that the Yippies
              were planning to kidnap delegates, careen stolen gas trucks at
                             police stations and hotels
              plus poison the air conditioning at the convention center
                                and oodles of other malevolences

The Yippies did not deny it
                (nor did I, with all my access
                                to the media)
It was perhaps partly under the rubric of
                                "ink is ink"
or Abbie's concept of "spooking"
                as a kind of armchair put-on with menace
        that none of us even commented
        on the impossible logistics
                of stealth-doping the water.

Mike Royko in his bio of Daley, *Boss*, said
the Chi Red Squad gathered every ridiculous rumor
and passed it on to reporters as "unimpeachable fact"

I had my own little place
                in the rev-up
        with a piece I wrote for the undergrounds
        hurriedly
        while trying to finish
                the final recording and mixing
                of *It Crawled into My Hand, Honest*

    a list of plans the Yippies
    intended for Chicago,
    a work that doesn't give me much pride
                                decades later

    I predicted things like
                rewriting the Bill of Rights
    plenty of balling and dope,
    a Yippie Ecological Conference,
    and dawn ass-washing ceremonies
                prior to Yippie volleyball tournaments.

In this rev-up toward violence
we later sniffed the secret emissions
of CIA CHAOS
        Army and maybe Naval Intelligence
in what they later openly called
                                psy-war

174

(except in Chicago
             it was more war and less psy)

By the beginning of August
I was afraid of the secret police
        whose moany shoves
                 like subsurface Blake-clanks
        I felt in my soul

This much I knew
        by the time of Chicago:
             When you rip the veil from Evil
             Evil rips back

In the search for a mantram
             to quell the violence
We finally settled on OM
Ginsberg and I published
             a statement
        in the "Convention Special" edition of
             RAT Subterranean News
        a few thousand of which were passed around
                                in Chicago:

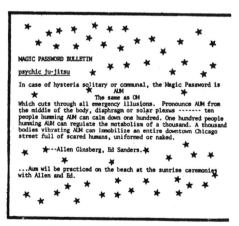

The Magic Password is Aum

Tuesday August 20
     Gov Sam H. Shapiro of Illinois

called up the national guard
                    at the snarl of Daley

Early in the AM on Thursday, August 22
                two teenage hippies
                near Lincoln Park
            were stopped by the police
            one was a Native American from South Dakota
            named Dean Johnson
They said he pulled a gun on him
They killed him with three shots

                        This was the horrid early
                        indication of Daley's fist

It was on my mind
when I arrrived in Chicago from L.A.
                        later that day
        as a kind of advance scout
                I had promised the Fugs
                        a safe place to stay

        Phil Ochs had a room at the Hilton
                        with the McCarthy campaign

    Abbie and Jerry chided him,
                but with RFK gone, McCarthy was the one for Phil

    There was a Yippie Snake Dance practice
            which sent fake shudders
                through the Mil-ints
                        and picked up a ridiculous amount of ink.

    There was a climate
    of police state experimentation
            that came into play in the days before the convention
                        —equipment, tactics, techniques—
    as the secret police, the FBI, the CIA, the Chicago police,
    Daley, Army Intelligence, et al
                betrayed their eagerness for pizza street

FRIDAY AUGUST 23

'Candidate' corralled

Yippie pigs in pokey

Ted to skip convention, aide says

It was a touching reunion. Pigasus oinked. Mrs. Pigasus squealed.

The pigs touched noses and then like any couple, went to opposite corners of their cage and ignored each other.

The pigs were reunited Friday night at the Anti-Cruelty Society, 157 W. Grand, after police "arrested" them in two separate Yippie demonstrations.

THE YIPPIES, members of the Youth International Party, say that Pigasus is their candidate for president, competing against anyone the Democrats might nominate next.

Pigasus was taken into custody Friday when he was caught on a leash by seven policemen as they tried to enter Plaza. Police also corral the pig.

the aides include folk singer Phil Ochs, 27, and Jerry Rubin, 30, a Yippie leader.

Pigasus was picked up when the Yippies gathered in Lincoln Park. His taunted a dozen authorities there tightened.

Yippie Mascot Pigasus (left) and mate reunited.

as they tried to security when they heard the corral the pig. Yippies would release greased pigs in the lobby.

Finally, one of the officers wrestled the pig into captivity.

THE EARLIER Civic Center foray spawned rumors at the Federal Building and gave them.

WITH THE two pigs in the pokey, the Yippies have threatened to release greased pigs all over the city.

"Somebody has offered to give us a whole farm full of pigs," one of them said.

Daily News Wire Services

WASHINGTON—Sen. Edward M. Kennedy (D-Mass.) does not plan to attend the Democratic National Convention.

A press aide said Kennedy plans to remain at the family compound at Hyannis Port, Mass., throughout the week.

Meanwhile, Alabama State. Sen. Thomas Radney said Chicago Friday that he second the presidential nomination of Kennedy.

Former Ohio Gov. Michael V. DiSalle said earlier that will place the senator's name before the convention. Kennedy has said that he is candidate.

Rooms at a Chicago have been reserved for members of the Kennedy who do attend the convention.

Kennedy aide

Ribicoff ready to back McGovern

Ribicoff, once John

who strongly urged to enter the race. McGovern the endorse Connecticut's 35 of the President

RIB

---

*A clipping that lay in my files
for 28 years*

The Yippies held a press conference
        at the Chicago Civic Center
to introduce
      the candidate known as Pigasus

Anita and Abbie had purchased
        a petite pig at a nearby farm
and in one of the stupidest
      quarrels in the history of the
             American left
Rubin felt that the Hoffmans' oinker
          was way too cute
that Pigasus had to be mean and tough
          A Street Fighting Pig

177

so that a more fierce and macho pig was purchased
and brought to the conference.

Just before it began
a person came up to a woman in the crowd,
handed her a shopping bag
and said, "Give that to Jerry Rubin."

Then he precipitously split
The woman opened it
and saw that it was packed with grass
She tossed it aside
    Then Pigasus arrived
        Rubin was holding it
            and speaking on its behalf
when the fuzz moved in.

Some officers shouted "Get Rubin, Get Rubin!"
Rubin denied he'd ordered
           a delivery of marijuana
                at the Pigasus conference
(You don't have grass delivered to a place
              surrounded by police)

"They seemed disappointed
that all they could charge me with
        was disorderly conduct,"
      he told a reporter.

Besides Rubin, the police arrested Phil Ochs
              and five others
and carted Pigasus away.
After that there was a 24 hour guard
        on the pigs at the Lincoln Park children's zoo

honk honk
go the geese of Canada

    That day
        Miriam and Deirdre, then 3½
                flew from New York

We stayed at the Lincoln Hotel
        on the edge of the park
                in Rm 817
We reserved 620 for Allen Ginsberg
        who arrived on Saturday the 24th

Country Joe and Fish played
        the Electric Circus that weekend
A few of us left in the middle of a meeting
      to confront Joe leaving the theater
           The Fugs and the Fish
          along with the MC5
              were the only rock bands
              still ready to come

McDonald told Abbie
they couldn't do it
The vibes in Chicago were too vicious
They were worried about their fans also
         and wanted their symbolic
         support withdrawn

The Fish went to their motel
       and were assaulted by
          three guys with crew cuts,
apparently from the South Carolina
Democratic delegation. Arr harr!

Wavy Gravy and the Hog Farm
      also refused to come to Chicago from New Mexico
again because of no permits
      and concern about the

Rubin/Hoffman/Yippie
peace/pizza street commixture

That Friday night
while we were nervously
settling into the teargas mode

Janis and Jimi
were talking in the dressing room
of the Singer Bowl in Queens
before going on
sharing some Jack Daniels

They were talking about the blues
when Jimi pulled out a Confederate flag
and blew his nose with it

to Janis' high pitched growly laugh
waiting to sing to the thousands

Saturday August 24

After a gathering in Rm 817
the Hotel Lincoln front desk
called, they wdn't let us have Yippies
in our room
for meetings

Hiss Hiss
go the secret police

That afternoon there was a big planning meeting
at the Free Theater at 1848 Wells
near the park

The police
were going to toss people
out at 11 pm
and no sleeping in the park

The issue was what to do

       Abbie predicted
          "fifty or sixty people in a band
          going out from the park to
          loot and pillage if they
               close it up at 11."

I didn't dig the L. & P. words
so I exploded, as they say,
"I'm sick and tired
of hearing people talk like that.
       I don't want some kid
who hasn't been through it all
and doesn't know what it's all about
going to get his head busted
You're urging people
      to go out and get killed
             for nothing
Man, that's like murdering people."

       We decided not to urge people
       to try to sleep in the park overnight
       though that was what was
             clearly going to happen

After Saturday afternoon's meeting
wherever Miriam, Didi and I went in Chicago
we were followed by two plainclothes detectives

       All the so-called leaders
          had surveillance teams.
       At the time I didn't think much of it
       I'm more angry about it now, decades later,
              than then.

That night Miriam, Didi and I walked from the Hotel Lincoln
       to a Mexican restaurant
          & the police waited outside
             to save Western Civ

Sunday August 25
The Festival of Life Begins
& the Democratic Convention

I'd found a safe place for the Fugs to stay
                                during the blood
but one of them phoned
from his room at the Tropicana in L.A.
They were worried about violence in Chicago

He said they'd seen a report on TV
that Country Joe
            had been punched out in a motel

They were hesitant to come

I was just a little bit angry
        but I remembered how embarassed I had been
                at the dawn Stony Brook concert
                        at having no current political tunes

so I left it up to them &
Tuli flew to Chicago, the rest to New York City.

Sunday was the opening of the Convention
with a "Welcoming of the Delegates"
                            at the downtown hotels

According to Norman Mailer
        Daley was looking to get Ted Kennedy
                to run against Humphrey
                    then if he lost
        to accept VP nomination under Hubert
        but if TK won
            Daley could take credit
                        for Humph-sweep-out

                The secret police had monitored
                plane, train and bus reservations

to Chicago
and knew the numbers
weren't high.

Daley had won.
Won it for Nixon

There were only about 5 to 6 thousand demonstrators
Daley had 6,500 National guardsmen
plus 6,000 soldiers
and 1,000 undercover agents

Military intelligence
told CBS
that 1 out of 6 protestors
in Chicago were government spies.

SATELLITES ABOVE THE PARK?

The CIA admitted later using
its satellites to spy on protestors
The cameras were positioned
over 100 miles high
and could focus on objects the
size of a suitcase

I wonder
if a CIA satellite were focussed
on Lincoln Park
that Sunday morning while a bunch of us
set things up in Lincoln Park
We did it quickly
as a kind of Digger fantasyland

There was a "Free Store" area
Some peace-balloons we dangled from trees
and a place for medical care

Sunday was also the "Day of the Honey"
Abbie introduced me to a guy
whom he called "Jim Morrison"•

who was dipping into jars of hash-oiled honey
                    with a spoon
          which he would swirl upon our tongues

It was very, very, very powerful
I looked up through the teargas sonata of Lincoln Park
and the Universe
               from the edge of the Lake
                         up across the wide Midwest sky
was made up of pulsing, writhing, and sift-shifting
                    mountains and vistas of Spinach

I was literally that: spinach! Cooked spinach.
It was as if I had awakened in one of my Kansas City aunt's
                              Thanksgiving dinner bowls!

I was not alone
My cofounder of the Fugs, Tuli Kupferberg,
had taken a tongue of the honey
                    and immediately passed out
Paul Krassner
was on his knees nearby
          holding on
      to the grass very tightly
            "so that I wouldn't fall up"
                         he later wrote

all of which made it difficult for us to
attend to the details of the imminent concert
                         by the MC5•

Unfortunately,
the police were not allowing the flat bed truck that
Abbie had rented for a stage
          into the park

so when the bard John Sinclair and his band arrived
they drove their van directly upon the grass
                         and we discussed what to do.

They parked near a little building
          so that the extension cord from their sound

system could reach a socket at the
side of the building

It took all my years of studying Greek and
silent languages
All my many months of handling complicated tours
with the Fugs
to focus through the Ultimate Spinach
and insert the MC5's sound plug
into the socket.

That was it—the structure of
Chicago city cooperation
with the Festival of Life:

one socket, one plug-in, one act

The MC5 had a flag draped over their amp stack
as they performed their
wall-of-sound
ultra high energy set
then they packed & drove out of Lincoln Park
toward their next gig.

I found my police surveillance team,
told them I wasn't feeling well
I did not mention the universal sea of Ultimate Spinach
in which we were standing

and they helped me back
to the Hotel Lincoln
till the waning of the Green

The bard Allen Ginsberg
recalls,
"A lot of us were wandering around Lincoln Park"
when police showed up with guns and clubs
"Nobody knew why or if the police were going to attack"

Ginsberg saw that some of the protestors
were ready to fight:

"Some of the Maoists were acting insulting
and revolutionary in their ideological prophetic style.
Police fear everywhere so I sat down and began chanting OM.
I thought I'd chant for about 20 minutes
and calm myself down,
            but the chanting stretched into hours
            and a big circle surrounded me."

He opened a small harmonium
and chanted six straight hours, till 10 PM

There was a dusky sundown
            in Lincoln Park
                        and the lights in the Hancock building
                                                switched on
            as the ommmer ommmed onward
            and the police announced
                        through loudspeakers
                                    the 11 pm curfew

By evening I had recovered from the Spinach
It was very very dark in Lincoln Park
            but we strolled among the clusters of Yippie campers
I had a walky talky to talk with others.
but, ai yi yi, I heard a voice over the speaker say,
                        "This is Ed Sanders
                        please join me by the zoo!"
                                    I shouted, "No! No!
                                    I'm not at the zoo!"

Allen and I banded together
            to lead people out of the park at 11
                        to avoid the whacking clubs
            I settled my tenor harmony
                        above his baritone
            and we brought a few hundred with us
                                    out of the hell

Earlier some had joined a march south
to the hotels in the loop
            such as the Hilton and Sheraton
            where many Democratic delegates were staying

There was no violence at the loop
but when the Yippies came back to Lincoln Park,
        out of the TV klieglights
                the police assaulted the demonstrators

There were about 1,000 in the park
                when the police began clubbing
                        some fought back
                                but most just bled

The police tore everything up
        smashed the Free Store
                seized the Yippie walky talkies
                        and drove everyone into the streets

They gleefully searched out reporters to club.
65 journalists were injured or arrested or had their equipment
                        smashed that night

The billyclubbers chased
        the tentative revolutionaries
                through the streets of nearby Old Town

and the outrage and the size of the crowds grew
                as night after night of police rampage continued.

Honk honk
go the geese of Canada

MONDAY AUGUST 26

There were about twenty of us
in the Hotel Lincoln coffee shop

At first they refused to serve us

"Is it money?" I asked, "You think we have no money?"
and I pulled about $2,000 in tens and twenties from
        my jeans
                and piled them high

near the salt and pepper

"Money talks now
    and who cares about later!?"
        the capitalists say
            and it talked loud enough
    that police-riot morn
        to get us served

I brought Didi and Miriam some breakfast
                        up to our room
and then we tried to take Deirdre
                across the park to the zoo
    but the gas still lingered in the grass
                and her eyes teared with the pain of it

That afternoon
I went with Miriam and Didi
    to the sporting goods section
        at Marshall Field's department store
where I was trying on football helmets
I wanted one with a face guard
            in case my police escort
                should wax face-bashy

and the tall plainclothes guy approached
He said, "Mr. Sanders, we've been following you for twelve hours,
and the next shift is scheduled to take our place.
I've called them. They'll be here in a few minutes.
If we miss them, it could be another six hours
                    before we're relieved."

I chuckled, and told him we'd wait

        Early in the evening
        I went back into the Lincoln Park
        I noticed, with a shudder, that
                my police escort
                were lifting billy clubs
                    out of their unmarked car

That night when the Yippies tried to march on the Loop
from Lincoln Park
     a line of army troops stopped them after a few blocks
          with an armored vehicle
               wrapped in barbed wire

    Barricades were built in Lincoln Park
        to defend the right to sleep there
   at 12:30 AM the police
        clubbed and attacked the barricades

          Jean Genet was in the park!
          He had no visa
             and had sneaked in from Canada
          Allen Ginsberg was acting as
             his interpreter
          Genet had an assignment for
          Esquire Magazine (along with Ginsberg,
          William Burroughs and Terry Southern)
            to cover the convention.

          All four had passes to attend the convention

"Not if it means violence"
        Ginsberg said
        when someone asked if he
            intended to remain in the park

    It was just about time for
        the invasion of the fuzz
    Tonight they marched behind
        a street sweeper truck whose
           water nozzles had been
        converted to spray tear gas

    (These ghastly police state devices
     maybe gifts from Garden Plot or the CIA Chaos program?)

    To me this was the last mote of proof
        in 1968
           that the Nation was lost

I'll never forget the sight of
Jean Genet, dressed in leather,
peering into the paranoid darkness
of the park just before the
                        fascist tear-gas trucks
            began their voyages of filth

He strode into the darkness
                        and was gassed

There were plenty of clergy on hand
and medical volunteers

While Ginsberg chanted OM
        for soothe-quell
    I heard a prominent Yippie
                do a counterchant
                        "Ommmmm sucks!
                        Ommmmmm is bullshit!"

Ginsberg said
        "I got gassed chanting AUM
                with a hundred youthful voices
                        under the trees…

        The Daily Mayor has written a
    bloody vulgar script for American Children."

I went with Allen back to the Hotel Lincoln
but there were snout-nozzled cops there
                lobbing tear-gas grenades
which plomfed near our feet
We crouched down and dashed through
                        the hostile molecules
heads low, knees high
        as if we were halfbacks
                on a high school football team

toward the lobby.
I later visited Allen in his room

where a nervous Burroughs
                    sat in ridicule

(The next day, Burroughs, Ginsberg, Genet and
Southern wrote a joint statement
                    about the police state riots
                        with Burroughs leading it off:

"Regarding conduct of police in clearing Lincoln Park
of young people assembled there for the purpose of
sleeping in violation of a municipal ordinance. The
police acted like vicious guard dogs attacking everyone
in sight. I do not 'protest.' I am not surprised. The
police acted after the manner of their species. The point
is why were they not controlled by their handlers? Is
there not a municipal ordinance requesting that vicious
dogs be muzzled and controlled?
                    Colonel William S. Burroughs")

Meanwhile the police, with knives and nightsticks,
sabotaged about 30 cars,
                    according to the *Chicago Journalism Review*
in the Lincoln Park lot
        all the cars had McCarthy stickers
        three or four flat tires on each, busted windows
                    broken aerials.

TUESDAY AUGUST 27

At dawn on the 27th
        the Yippies promised
                    "poetry, mantras, religious ceremony"
on the shore of Lake Michigan

I slept late
        but Ginsberg was there in the park
singing various mantras
                    for several hours
till his voice became hoarse and whispery
                        from overommming.

The Yippies and the Mobe
threw a 60th unbirthday party
that night for Lyndon Johnson
            at the packed Chicago Coliseum
1513 So. Wabash

They asked me to be the m.c.
and so I scurried
        back and forth between backstage
and the microphone
            making sure it went by
                    in one smooth flow
Six thousand people were there
A band called Home Juice
            opened with a 20 minute set.
The duo called Jim and Jean sang.
While Phil sang "I Ain't Marchin' Anymore"
a guy burned his draft card
and then in one amazing sequence of seconds
there was a sudden poof-up of
                maybe a hundred blazing draft cards
        pointillisticly patterning
                    the Coliseum audience

The great Dave Dellinger spoke, and
Dick Gregory, and Jean Genet

I auctioned off the original statement
            signed by Burroughs, Genet, Ginsberg, Southern
                to help bail people out

Ginsberg's voice had not yet returned
            from his many hours
                of chanting
                    to quell the violence
so he passed me a note to read
            to the audience:

(Introduce me as Prague King of May—Ed—in my turn,
you explain I lost my voice chanting Aum in park—so please
you read my piece—then I'll do 3 Minutes of <u>Silence</u> Mind
consciousness & belly)

The honorable Pigasus was brought forward
      and Paul Krassner was his interpreter
At another point
Abbie Hoffman, not scheduled to speak
           nevertheless trotted onto the stage
                and grabbed the microphone

At the end of this fine affair
we sang happy unbirthday to the napalm man
        and it was back out to the
                blood bash boulevards

Demonstrators were chased from Lincoln Park
           with Daley's sleazy teargas trucks

There was a march out of the park
        toward the Dem Conv
           at the International Ampitheatre
but after ten blocks
        stopped by a line of soldiers
and a grim police-state vehicle

ringed with barbed wire
and outfitted with rotating searchlights!

Hoffman lay down
in front of it
and gave it the finger

Police filled Michigan Ave
by the Conrad Hilton hotel,
and Grant Park just across the Street

Around 1:30 am the police announced
that demonstrators could stay in Grant Park
if they stayed "peaceful"

At 3 am the National Guard relieved
the Chicago police at the Hilton

WEDNESDAY AUGUST 28

The ghastly word inked forth that
George Corley Wallace was on the ballot in 43 states
He was coming back from a western tour
and headed toward the South

and at dawn around 80 protestors
remained in front of the Hilton

That afternoon
Daley had allowed
a single rally at the bandshell
in Grant Park
sponsored by the Mobilization

From 10 to 15,000 showed up

Daley had turned down a permit
to march to the Convention
The Mobe announced it would try it anyway

Wed Afternoon is when the convention
          voted down a peace platform plank
          1,567¾ to 1,041½

When Phil Ochs heard the news
     he sensed the Fall of America
          and Bloody Wednesday began

     Some protestors had canteens
          and pieces of cloth to wetten
     I had purchased a few dozen daisies
          to use as a gas mask
     I handed some out to friends

William Burroughs Holding Some of My Gas Mask Daisies•

     At the Grant Park bandshell
     there were speeches and songs

     And then at 3
     a Chicago police undercover officer
     posing as a biker
     led a charge
          to pull down an American flag from its staff

With him were some guys
            who wanted to run the
                        black cloth of Anarchia
                                    up the stanchion
—proper for the city of the Haymarket riot

                        (The "biker" had volunteered
                        to be Jerry Rubin's bodyguard
                        and Rubin was apparently flattered
                        that a prole from the urban underworld
                                    had come to him
                                                on the shores of wierdness)

Police fired teargas
            protestors lobbed it back
      and there were clubbings and arrests

            Rennie Davis was beaten bloody
            The blood soaked rag
                        with which his wound was stanched
            was later run up the
                        Grant Park pole

            Tom Hayden
                        spoke to the crowd suggesting that
                        people break up into small groups
                                    and go out into the streets

                        (Things were happening also at
                          Lincoln Park
                          Rubin had arranged for Bobby Seale
                                      to give a speech there
                          the basis for Seale's later
                                      indictment with the Chicago 8)

About 4:30
Dave Dellinger addressed the crowd
            through a portable bull horn
      to announce a nonviolent march to the Democratic Convention
            4½ miles

from Grant Park

Grant Park is connected to downtown via a series of bridges
                    across railroad tracks to the west
Lines of soldiers prevented the march from leaving
                                over any of the bridges
U.S. Army helicopters circled overhead

It was very scary
            There were fixed bayonets
            & jeeps with barbed wire
                            hippie-sweeping screens
            plus the whoppa whoppa
                            of helicopters
            that mixed with the songs Phil Ochs
            sang to calm us:

        "We're the cops of the world, boys,
        We're the cops of the world...."
                    & then his song,
            "Outside of a Small Circle of Friends"

singing through the bullhorn
                    someone was holding to his face
so that his guitar could not be heard
                    while Dellinger
            went off to talk with the police

Then Allen Ginsberg,
            still hoarse from singing seed syllables
                            in the rings of violence
            chanted "The Grey Monk" of William Blake

through the bull horn

All of us who were sitting and waiting
were chatty and restless
yet by the time he chanted
  the final verses of the wounded Gray Monk
all was silent
  except the ghastly helicopters:

"Thy Father drew his sword in the North,
With his thousands strong he marched forth;
Thy Brother has arm'd himself in Steel
To avenge the wrongs thy Children feel

"But vain the Sword & vain the Bow,
They never can work War's overthrow.
The Hermit's Prayer & the Widow's tear
Alone can free the World from fear.

"For a Tear is an Intellectual Thing,
And a Sigh is the Sword of an Angel King,
And the bitter groan of the Martyr's woe
Is an Arrow from the Almightie's Bow.

"The hand of Vengeance found the Bed
To which the Purple Tyrant Fled;
The iron hand crush'd the Tyrant's head
And became a Tyrant in his stead."

I was sitting down on the sidewalk with
Terry Southern, William Burroughs and Jean Genet
in front of the rifle-poking soldiers

  A few of us had pushed fresh daisies
  into the rifle barrels at the Pentagon
    just 10 months ago
  and now, even though
    I again had fresh white flowers
  I knew this was a different type of event
    and that I would likely have been
      bayonetted and shot
     pushing petal in metal

Finally, after hours of negotiations,
    the protestors found a way
                of getting out of Grant Park
  and they surged
      across a bridge
        & gathered in front of the Hilton
                on Michigan Avenue at Balbo

Others walked miles north or south
to get around the National Guard on the bridges

In the lobby where the Democrats
prepared to go to the convention hall
                four miles away
soldiers with helmets & guns
        marched past the plush divans
               & the potted trees

      Medical teams began to arrive
      from local medical schools
      and from the Chicago chapter of the
          Medical Committee for Human Rights

      A few thousand gathered on Michigan
          in front of the huge Hilton
      or they stood at a gas-avoiding distance
              on the edge of the park

Then, without warning, a throng of police charged the
demonstrators at 7:56
      smashing, macing, beating
      apparently to clear the avenue

Ten minutes later the protestors were back
    chanting
        "What do we Want?
        Peace!
        When do we want it?
        Now!"

    Jeeps with machine guns mounted to them
    arrived at the Hilton

Just then a mule wagon pulled onto Michigan Avenue
from the Poor People's Campaign
                    a police officer fired tear gas at it
            Welcome to Chicago
                        said the sign

Some leaped behind the Poor People's mule train,
led by Ralph Abernathy
            which had a permit to go to the convention hall.

"Wahoo! Wahoo!"
            like the bomb-riding cowboy
                in Dr. Strangelove
shouted an officer on a three wheeled motorcycle
as he mashed into the crowd

The bar at the Hilton
                was named after the Haymarket riot
                        of 1886
                            police against anarchists

It was packed with reporters
People outside came crashing through the window
The police then leaped through the broken glass
                            to beat those trying to flee
They still seemed particularly eager to
                        bash reporters.

Thus began hours of bloodshed
In the streets outside the Hilton and Convention Center
It was a place of 10,000 anecdotes
as the police nightsticked, hurled tear gas, bludgeoned
                            and made blue red—
Among their victims was a crippled bystander

                and it was there
                in the surgery-room glare of the television lights—
                that thousands took up the chant
                        "The whole world is watching
                            the whole world is watching...."

McCarthy volunteers set up
a first aid station on the Hilton's 15th floor
                                        at his suite
They gave up their passes
                to get the injured up to the room

Humphrey was on the 25th floor
        An aide opened a window and complained
                        of tear gas

On the nominating floor four miles from the Hilton
CBS-TV's Dan Rather gave a live report,
        "A security man just slugged me in the stomach,"
        to which Walter Cronkite replied,
                        "I think
                        we've got a
                        bunch of thugs here,
                        Dan."

Inside the convention that horrible night
Senator George McGovern was a last minute peace candidate
after McCarthy refused to lead a floor fight
                                against Humphrey•

Senator Abraham Ribicoff was giving his nominating speech:
"With George McGovern," said Ribicoff, "we wouldn't have Gestapo
tactics on the streets of Chicago."

Mayor Richard Daley, his face reddened with malevolence,
shouted, "Fuck you, you Jew son of a bitch!
                You lousy motherfucker, go home!"

Daley was seated in the front
                Ribicoff looked down at Red Face, and said
                        "How hard it is to hear the truth."

When a Wisconsin delegate asked
                        stood up and asked the convention
                to adjourn itself for two weeks
                                because of the beatings in the street
                Allen Ginsberg leaped to his feet in the balcony

and began shouting "OMMMMM" for about five minutes•

Meanwhile, outside
            in the television lights
the teargassed, terrified and angry crowd
continued its own version of ommmmm,
"The Whole World is Watching!
            The Whole World is Watching!"

Hubert Humphrey picked up the nomination
on the first ballot:
        Humphrey 1761¾
        McCarthy   601
        McGovern   146½

It was reported that Humphrey
            lurched up from his seat
                in his suite
                    and kissed the television set
when he "went o'er the top"

    A day or two later, according to an Army record,
    Warren Christopher (later Secretary of State, but
    then a Deputy United States Attorney General)
    called the Pentagon and asked for still
    and motion pictures taken by a
                U.S. Army Intelligence unit
        of demonstrators outside the Convention

YEATS IN THE GAS

    Phil Ochs later mentioned how
    in the horror of the gas and the clubs
    he thought of Yeats

"I was in the worst police brutality," he said, "right when they charged
up by the Hilton. I was between the charging cops and the crowd and I
raced into a doorway in the nick of time.... While racing away from the
tear gas, I just had a sensation of Yeats. I thought of Yeats (laughs) for
some reason."

I wondered about that for years
till it dawned that he might
have been thinking of Yeat's poem
"Easter 1916"

and its repeated line
A terrible beauty is born

That is, those crazy youth and not-so-youth
their hasty signs, their hasty props, their
hasty yells
were transformed in the
Chicago injustice
so that
A terrible beauty was born

"Chicago has no government,"
said Allen Ginsberg a few weeks later.
"It's just anarchy maintained by pistol. Inside the
convention hall it was rigged like an old Mussolini strong-arm
scene—police and party hacks everywhere illegally, delegates
shoved around and kidnapped, telephones lines cut."

and, in opposing it,
A terrible beauty was born

I was in a "don't say hello/don't say goodbye"
mood
and wanted to get out of the hell of Chicago
to the safety of Avenue A
where the street-sweeping trucks
still used water

It all seemed so senseless
I filed away the clips I cut
of the action in Chicago
the leaflets and fliers
and let them rest in a box for 28 years

The Fugs decided to
tour wherever possible with Pigasus

In early September I wrote a
            Prayer for the Pig
hoping to use it, not as a poem,
                but as a chant or a song:

            "We
            pray for the pig
            confused and surrounded by hate-vectors

            pray for the pig
            in the missions of nausea & gas

            pray for the greed-pig
            lost among money need & ledgers

            pray for the war-pig
            riving & cursing in
            foam-fits of war

            pray for the glory-pig
            licking the leather of fame
            with snout snorkles & pig gobble

            pray for the poet-pig
            slobbering for the laurel,
            grappling the sunshine,
            lusting for acceptance
            with a string of words in the void

            pray for the silence-pig
            lost in lonerhood
            while pregnant women bleed to death
            in the alleys of the poor

            We
            pray for the lost grey honkie
            surly & despising,
            lost in comfortland
            of self & family & money....

            Onward Earthlings, kiss the radiance,
            worship yourselves, & pray for the pig."

I might have chanted some o' this prayer at every gig
or used it as the Mantram I did not sing
                              in Lincoln Park
but I didn't
        It lurked in my files
                        till time for this book

FIRING LINE

September 3
    the day after my
                prayer for the pig
    I was on William Buckley's television show
    Firing Line with Jack Kerouac and sociologist Lewis Yablonsky
    author of a book called *The Hippie Trip*

        I was in the elevator
        going up to the studio
        when a guy came in
                    in a checked jacket
        with two friends

        I didn't recognize him at once
        All of sudden he said,

        "You look like Ginsberg
        You talk like Ginsberg
        & You write like Ginsberg"

    Then a prosopognosis with a jolt of thrill!
    One of my heroes
                whose novels
    especially *Big Sur, Dharma Bums* and *The Subterraneans*
            had been like religious texts
                    when I was in college

    I knew he'd swung to the right,
                    as they say,
    and was supporting Buckley's run for mayor of NYC

He'd ridden to NY with two pals
                    Joe Chaput and Paul Bourgeois

They'd had a couple of drinks on arriving in NYC
then checked into the Delmonico Hotel. Burroughs was also
at the Delmonico, finishing his piece on Chicago for *Esquire*

Jack chugged and smoked pot
                    into the zonk mode
Burroughs urged him not to go on the show

After the first segment
            his chair fell off the studio riser
                and it was obvious he was
                                stumbly-drunk
The producer wanted to substitute Allen Ginsberg
(who was in the audience) for Kerouac
but we all protested
            and on he went

I mentioned Ginsberg & Kerouac
                as heroes of my generation
            but Kerouac said
        "I'm not connected with Allen Ginsberg
                and don't you put my name next to his."

He wasn't very friendly
        his face very florid
            and his forehead vein popped out
                        when he stroked above his nose
                    with a hand that held
                                a coronella-sized cigar
I told him that I respected his writing too much
            and that I wasn't going to fight with him
                        on camera
even though my years steeped in controversy
            as a poet, publisher and Fug
            had trained me well
                to give back razory raillery—

I was very tempted to mention his daughter Jan
                who'd come to many Fugs shows
I remembered how the owner of the Astor Place Playhouse

206

had come upon Jan and a Fugs guitarist making it
            on the drum riser
                        one midnight
I remembered how Kerouac would call me now and then
            and recite little poems
                        which I would write down

I remembered other things
            that Peter Orlovsky told me
                        in Peace Eye
                                    after Kerouac visited Allen's pad
                                                just up the street at 408 E. 10th

but why tell all
            just because Tell tells you to tell?

                        and I kept silent
                                    in front of the author
                                    Mexico City Blues

Afterwards we all went out
            to a bar in Times Square
                        to light up the neon liver

On September 5
            the National Commission on
            Causes and Prevention of Violence
        said it would investigate
                        police violence in Chi

The next day
    Mayor Richard Daley
        issued his report
            that supported what his police
                        did during the Convention

September 6 & 7,
    the Doors played the London theater
                        called the Round House
                    The Fugs would be there later in the month

September 10
    I put out a press release on September 10
    about upcoming Fugs concerts in London and
    at the International Song Festival in Essen, Germany

    I mentioned we would be traveling with Pigasus

    and this: "After the Essen Song Festival the
            Fugs will journey with Pigasus to the
            Czechoslovakian border and attempt to
            go to Prague where they intend to hold a free
            concert and poetry reading, meet with their brothers
            in the streets, and conduct a pilgrimage to the
            birthplace of Franz Kafka, an early Yippie."

In September, at last,
    It Crawled Into My Hand, Honest
                  was pressed, printed
               & distributed by Warner/Reprise!

September 13
    direct press censorship was reestablished in
                    in Czechoslovakia

and the next day
    Denny McClain
        won his 30th game
            as Detroit Tigers
                defeated the Oakland A's

By Mid September
    the U.S. had 535,000 troops in Nam

    & a group called Radical Women protested the
                    Miss America pageant
                      in Atlantic City
    They auctioned off a Miss America dummy
    set up a "freedom ashcan"
        tossed bras, girdles, dishcloths, and steno pads

though it was always the burned & banished bras
that titillated the curve-batty media
and not the dishcloths & pads

From September 9–14
the Fugs went back to Montreal
to play again at the New Penelope•

The local underground paper helped us
rent a candidate

We went with Pigasus
to the U.S. Consulate
w/ a CBC film crew
The Consulate officials
lied later,
saying we'd had the pig wrapped in an
American flag

Actually
it was covered with a gunny sack

The footage was to be
broadcast alongside
a Moral Rearmament program.

On September 15 in Montreal
I bought a tiny electronic synthesizer
called a Stylophone
the beginning for me of what I called the
E/B/S, or Electronic Bard System

I began turning tiny synthesizers
into instruments
with keyboards mounted to garden gloves
called the Pulse Lyre

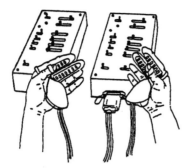

and followed
over the years by the Talking Tie,
the Singing Quilting Frame, the Microlyre
the Lisa Lyre
        and the Bird Lyre

In Sweden an important election September 15
The Social Democrats had been in power
                for 36 years
and the right wing hoped to trounce
but the Soc Dems won

The '68 election was
        the last for the two-chamber system
to be replaced in '71
        with a single

The goal of the Social Democrats
was for the State
to own 25% of industry
        Sweden had formed a state-owned bank
        which could give low-interest loans
        to businesses
        in exchange for the right to purchase stock
            in the companies it aided

& a value-added tax
was created
      instead of retail sales tax
            for 1-1-'69

September 20
The U.S. military
swore upon a stack of
fragmentation grenades
that "defoliation in South Vietnam had produced no harmful results."

The next day the Soviets sent Zond 5
around the moon
& resecured it
after an Indian Ocean plop.

On 9-24
two FBI agents visited our house
on Avenue A
I let them in, but restricted the questions.
Later when I received some of my files
through the Freedom of Information Act,
I saw what they wrote:
"Outside of his personal belongings the only items he took with him to
Chicago were five dozen daisies and a gas mask."

Perhaps they were looking for the origins of the psychedelic honey
or maybe they felt I would break down sobbing
to admit
I hauled in
a crate of
bazookas packed in grease.

My FBI files indicate bureau awareness
that the Fugs were thinking
of trying to visit Prague•

A single entry remaining on a page otherwise totally censored
dated 9-25-68
to Director Hoover from SAC, New York:
"Ed Sanders hoped to leave for Prague, Czechoslovakia, on 9/18/68."

Perhaps they felt I might
be going to pick up my rubles from the KGB

And so Miriam and I and the Fugs
                    flew to Europe for the second time
first to the Essen Song Festival
September 25–29
            with Frank Zappa and the Mothers
                            and many others

Once again,
            we held a press conference with Pigasus
                        this one in the central square of Essen

The Fugs did a concert or two
            appeared on a political panel
        and then did what we hungered to do
        tried to sneak in Czechoslovakia

We rented a car
            and drove toward Czechoslovakia—
                Ken Weaver, Miriam, myself
                        and Peter Edmiston,
                                of Edmiston-Rothschild Management

        We couldn't go through East Germany
        So we drove southwest into Bavaria
                            to the Czech border

        In a restaurant in Bavaria
                I wrote much of a song called
        "Jimmy Joe the Hippybilly Boy"
                        which I later recorded on *Sanders Truckstop*

        It was potato harvesting season
        and we spotted big carts of potatoes
                                in distant fields
                        right at the border

        We heard that at harvest
        farm workers
                cross back and forth across the border
                        along farm roads

            so we thought we might sneak

                    along a potato lane
               then streak to Prague

          We had some vague concept
          of shooting an album cover
                         lying down in front of the Soviet tanks
          and to visit the the house of Kafka,
          whose texts seemed keys to quelling the fear
                              at the end of an
                                        endless year

          We tried going in by one of the paved roads
          They were stopping even the milk trucks

          While we waited
          Miriam walked out into a field
                         to pick some small light yellow wild violas
          next to the border guard
          We pressed them along with little blue harebells and clover
                                        in a poetry book
          Here's the harebell-viola glyph
                    still resting in the
                         bound copy of *Peace Eye*

          Then we drove along the potato wagon border
          looking for a guardless path
                         to Czechoslovakia
               We thought we had found one

A few more yards and we'd have been
                              on the way to Prague
but then we spotted
            a single guard
with a machine gun hanging down his back
                              off a shoulder strap
"Halten sie!" he shouted,
holding out his weapon,
                and then gave forth
                a stream of German
                        ending with "demonstrazionen"

Miriam was asleep beneath a blanket
                        in our rented BMW
            and the guard thought we were trying
                              to smuggle her in

and thus came to closure
                our search for an album cover
                        with Soviet tanks

On Monday September 30
the Fugs flew to England
            for television
                and some concerts

That day we had a press reception
at the Arts Laboratory on Drury Lane

Tuesday October 1•
            We were on the BBC TV show
                        "Twenty Four Hours"
                at Lime Grove
                Shepherds Bush

We got a note that
the BBC producer was fairly eager
                to discuss our "programme content"

Friday October 4
　　　　Fugs on the BBC TV "How It Is"
　　　　Studio G, Lime Grove
　　　　a live show at 6 p.m.

　　　　and then to a gig at the
　　　　　　　　Roundhouse
　　　　　　　　Chalk Farm
　　　　　　　　Camden Town, London
It was the new theater
of the Institute of Contemporary Arts
A good place to play
The Doors and Jefferson Airplane
　　　　　　　　had been there not long before
& our opening act was the Hare Krishna singers.

We rented a double decker bus
　　　　　　for a trip to Stonehenge
We packed it full of friends
and were ready to
　　　　　　head for that remarkable circle of
　　　　　　　　　　　　　　　　　stones
but there was a bit of a delay
because a poet friend, Michael Horowitz
had a toothache
　　　　so we paused the bus
　　　　　　　　at his dentist

and then headed out over the flatlands to Wiltshire
It was before they shut it off from visitors
and we could clamber
　　　　　　upon the liths
　　　　　　　　in playful awe.

We flew back to New York
and then almost at once to Toronto
for an October 7 concert at Massey Hall
　　　　　　one of the best Fugs concerts of '68
but I've never seen a tape of it in the bootleg catalogs.

While we were in Europe
the jerks at the House Unamerican Activities Committee
subpoenaed Dave Dellinger of the Mobe,
        and Abbie and Jerry of the Yippies
            to give some testimony
                in D.C. on October 3

A U.S. marshal boarded a plane carrying Abbie
            from Chicago to N.Y.
                to serve him

Abbie's Subpoena to Appear before the
House Unamerican Activities Committee

It was scheduled as a three-day event
October 1 Mayor Daley et al gave their testimony
but October 2 was called off because of the
                              opening of the World Series
                                        Detroit vs. St. Louis

On the morning of October 3
Abbie arrived at the HUAC building
               with a smile on his face
                        wearing an American flag shirt
                        stars running vertical on the left
                        stripes down the right
                                        and wraparound shades

        The Capitol police arrested him on the steps
        A photograph of the time
                        shows a cop holding Abbie's elbow
               his forearm jutting upward
                        just before the shirt was removed
                                revealing a Vietcong flag painted
                                                on his back

                        (Of course now, decades thence
                                women in bikini catalogs
                                        shows patterns of flag
                                                on the mons veneris)

        Anita Hoffman flew to his aid
                just as she had in the Yip-In
                        and she was arrested also

        Yippie Brad Fox was arrested
                letting the air out of the left rear tire
                                of the patrol wagon
                                        with the Hoffmans inside

Inside the HUACery
a barefoot Jerry Rubin stood resplendent
               in three-quarter length velvet pantaloons
                        naked from the waist up
                                his neck adorned with a necklace

with a live ammo bandoleer
                    a toy M-16
and a beret completing his sartorial presentation.

When the undercover police officer
                    who had served as Rubin's tough guy
                            aide-de-freakout in Lincoln Park
(and who helped trigger the riot in Grant Park)

testified that Rubin had said, in the park on August 27,
                    "We should isolate one or two police and kill them."

Rubin shouted, "This worm's lies will prejudice my case in Chicago!"

Five lawyers for the "defendants"
            including William Kunstler
                    demanded to cross-examine the hostiles
            but were denied
                    and tossed from the room
                            when they stood in silent protest

The same day as HUAC
            George C. Wallace
            picked bomb-batty General Curtis LeMay
                    (the inspiration for
                    the mad general in Terry Southern's
                            Dr. Strangelove)
            to run with him as VP for the American Independent Party
            but the hate hicks erred
                    and began to lose support
            when at the October 3 press conference
            bonk-bonk LeMay said
                    he "would use anything that we could dream up,
                    including nuclear weapons, if
                            it was necessary"
                            to win the war.

"WHERE'S THE DEPRAVO DATA?" PART III

Hung up as always
                    with fucking, genitals, dope & assignations

FBI headquarters
sent another "airtel" message to its stations
                                    on October 9:

It reminded tardy agents that memos had
been spilled forth on May 10 and May 23
advising all FBI offices
"of the necessity of taking immediate action to expose,
disrupt, and otherwise neutralize the activities of the New Left. As a
part of this program, you were instructed to remain alert for and to
seek specific data depicting the depraved nature and moral looseness
of the New Left. You were further instructed to consider ways to use
this material in a vigorous and enthusiastic approach to neutralizing
them."

The FBI airtel went onward to beg
                                    for smut:

"Despite these instructions and in the face of mounting evidence
of their moral depravity,
            little evidence has reached the Bureau
            to indicate field offices
            are using this information to best advantage."

"...Where a student is arrested during a demonstration or his
participation in a demonstration is accompanied by the use of or
engagement in an obscene display, this information is to be promptly
incorporated into an anonymous letter which can be directed to his
parents."
            The airtel urged the Agents to include photos.

                    Nobody loves weirdness
                    more than the secret police.
                    It signs their paychecks.

October 10
        I was invited to speak at Iona College
        along with Paul Krassner, Abbie Hoffman
        and Black Panther Minister of Information
                    and presidential candidate for the

                                                    219

Peace and Freedom Party
                    Eldridge Cleaver

We spoke on the columned steps of one of the buildings
to a crowd of maybe a hundred.

Cleaver arrived with about 25
                    shudder-producing Panthers
and when it was his turn to speak
a priest, Iona faculty member Brother Edward Duggan
stood across from him
                    in front of another building &
          disrupted his words by shouting
          through a bull horn

Cleaver was fairly calm about it,
and quoted Voltaire's
"last priest strangled with the guts of the
                              last capitalist"

a startling string of words that had no results,
till the police
asked the college president
          —since, shudder shudder,
          ACTUAL Panthers were circulating in the audience
                    and things were hostile—
     to tell Bro Duggan to stop bullhorning
                         so that Cleaver could finish.

This whole event, including a photo of me,
is contained in a Senate Internal Security Subcommittee
report
     which reveals that a full array of FBI,
     Yonkers Red Squaders and assistant District Attorneys,
     monitored the event

and dutifully took down license plates in the parking lot
which the Internal Security committee published
                         in its report!•

NUX-545 N.J.
　Joseph Scheer, 527 Lexington Ave., Clifton, N.J. 1965 Plymouth Red Hard Top.
EN-2520 Conn.
　John J. Engretti, 17 Chambers St., Waterbury, Conn. 1960 VW—Yellow—2 Dr. Sed.
JA-871 Conn.
　Sergei C. Nutenoff. Old Town Rd., West Cornwall, Conn. 1959 VW—White Convertible.
BZ-5164 Conn.
　John Yopp. 53 Watson St., New Haven, Conn. 1966 VW—Brown 2 Dr. Sed.
906-498 VA.
　Alvin Louis Mente Jr., DOB 10-22-11. 165 Cameron News, Alexandria, Va., 1964 Buick Convertible.
6751 XE N.Y.
　Dorothy Harding, 1075 University Ave., Bronx, N.Y.C. Bus. Add.: R.H. Macy, 34th St., N.Y.C. 1962
Rambler Sed., Red.
RW-0324 N.Y.
　Thomas Keslovsky. 124th St., Brentwood, N.Y. Bus. Add.: Fordham University, Bronx, N.Y.C. 1965
Olds—Sed.—White.
LZ-7126 N.Y.
　Alexander Stevens. Box 312, Purling, N.Y. 1967 Olds 4 Dr. Maroon.
V-6371
　William A. Romano, 183 W. Hartsdale Ave., Hartsdale, N.Y. 1966 Buick Coupe. Tan.
SZ 7927
　Chrysler Leasing Corp., 341 Massachusetts Ave., Highland Park, Mich.
480-546 Mass.
　James W. O'Brien. 409 Kathleen Ave., Somerset, Mass. 1960 Cadillac, Blue, Convertible.
5396 GIT N.Y.
　Oscar Best, 4000 12th St., Long Island City. 1964 Ford Sed. Bus. Add.: Federal Reserve Bank, 23
Liberty St., N.Y.C. 1964 Ford, Sed. Red.
WM-8586
　William A. Graves. 535 6th Ave., New Rochelle, N.Y.1961 Chev., 2 Dr. Black.
2206 WH
　Ernest Ledermann, 123 Woodlawn Ave., New Rochelle, N.Y. 1967 Nash, Sedan. White—Bus. Add.:
N.Y. Life Ins. Co., 355 Lexington Ave., N.Y.C.
WD 7662
　Lloyd R. Goldson. 453 So. 7th Ave., Mt. Vernon, N.Y. 1967 Dodge, 2 Dr., Blue.
GW-5480
　Morris M. Stone. 1222 A. Midland Ave., Bronxville, N.Y. 1960 Cadillac, 2 Dr. Sedan.
　Eldridge Cleaver. 12-11-66. Iona College.
WH-7192
　James B. Priloff. 24 Cameron Pl., New Rochelle, N.Y. 1066 Plymouth, 4 Dr. Green.
TE-7061—Cleaver—1966 Ply. 4 Dr. Green. DOB 12-7-33.
　Glenda Gregory. 165 Clinton Ave., Brooklyn N.Y.C. Employed—Dept. of Correction, 100 Centre St.,
N.Y.C.—Since 1-27-66.
684 700—Guards
　Sanco Service Inc. 1225 President St., Brooklyn, N.Y.C. 1966 Dodge Taxi. Green & White.

For the preservation of America, they printed
the license plates of those at the Iona rally

That night of October 10
there was a benefit for the Catonsville 9
　　　　　　　　at the St. Mark's Church
I wish I had a time machine
　　　　　to go hang out and hear
Paul Blackburn, Ron Padgett, Kenneth Koch,
Joel Oppenheimer
　　　　　Ron Loewinsohn and Michael Palmer
　　　　　　　　　　raise a few hundred

THE FALL OLYMPICS

The Mexican government was vehement to
　　　　　　　　forge placid streets
　　　　　　　　　　even with blood
　　　because the language of the deal with
　　　the International Olympic Committee
　　　made clear the games could only be held
　　　　　　if the host country had a nice, docile populace

so in the weeks leading up to October

the army occupied the university in Mexico City
Over 50 people were killed
      and Chicago-like patrols surrounded Olympic stadium

Some remember the 15 days
in Mexico City
    for the Black Power gloves
        in the stadium

but the truth is that there were
so many
   good players
    in the Olympics
      the time-track
        could have used
          a Pindar
Jim Hines won 100 meter run
    in 9.89 seconds

   There was a great pole vault competition
   a three-way tie at 17′ 8⅝″

      with Bob Segren the winner
        because of fewer misses

In field hockey
   Pakistan beat Australia 2-1
      for the gold

A sixteen year old named Debby Meyer
    won the 200, 400, & 800 meter freestyle
        first places

There was a new technique
    called the Fosbury flop
      enabling Dick Fosbury
to win the high jump gold
   as he sailed over the bar
      on his back

    and many other
    Pindaric moments
      thirsting for meter

October 12
    saw the glorious moment
        of the raised fist glyph
when Tommy Smith
won the 200 meters
    in a world's record 19.8 seconds
        raising his arms in jubilance
& John Carlos winning the bronze.

A few minutes later
on the platform of triumph
Carlos and Smith both lifted their arms
    during the national anthem
        with fists enmeshed in black gloves

a glorious glyph that told the world
    such tales the War Caste forbade

    Both were dismissed
    from the squad
        by the U.S. Olympic Committee
           and sent home

October 18
        John and Yoko were busted at Ringo's pad
                by a sniff dog & seven fuzz
                        for grass
                                booked at police station
                        and later fined 150 pounds

and two days later
        Jackie and Aristotle married on Scorpios

The Living Theater
                had a three week run in October
                                at the Brooklyn Academy of Music
after four years of exile.

They did four plays
                including *Mysteries and Smaller Pieces*
I saw the performance
                of *Paradise Now*

        which began with communards
        strutting through the audience
        confronting people with

                "I cannot travel without my passport
                I do not know how to stop wars
                I cannot live without money
                I am not allowed to smoke marijuana
                I am not allowed to take off my clothes"

and then many stripped down to loin cloths
                as I watched from the side
                        with my scorchéd eyes

October 23
        finally! after months of
        debate-killing terror
        some right wing Cubans were
        arrested in New York
                for some of the bombings

Fugs   October 25   in Boston
                   once again at the Psychedelic Supermarket
                           for thrills and partying

A group called W.I.T.C.H.
for Womens International Terrorist Conspiracy from Hell
                   raided the New York Stock Exchange
                           and left behind hexes

November 2 Hendrix came out with
Electric Ladyland
           and it seemed like every
                   alternate wall in the nation
                               had his poster.

Humphrey staggered onward
in the fall campaign.
At first there were "ever present hecklers" at his stops.
           Anger-creating and frustrating—
                   maybe they were right wing
                               provocateurs for Tricky

        The hecklers began to lessen
                   as Hubert's campaign continued.

           I switched off my disgust
           & voted for him
           just as I had voted for Johnson in '64
                           after picketing the
                           Democratic Convention
                                   in Atlantic City
           on behalf of the seating of the
           Mississippi Freedom Delegation

           Humphrey would never have been able
                           to buck the War Caste
           and the image of him stupidly lurching
                       to kiss the tube in his room
                           in Chicago
               while the War Caste bloodied the streets

chilled my sight
                more than Yeats' cold cry to "cast a cold eye..."

THE SECRET POLICE GO AGAINST THE FUNDING OF THE UNDERGROUND PRESS

A CIA Chaos program analyst,
                saving western civ
                        by spending taxpayer's money
                                gazing at the underground press
came up with a simple strategy
                for the Secret Police
                        that "worked"

Much of Operation Chaos is stupidly still kept secret
It's known that the CIA began it in August of '67
and that much of its "work"
                was spying on and
                        looking for ways to
                                stymie the anti-war left—
The Underground Press was one of the Chaos program's targets

One of the Operation Chaos' programs
                        was called Project Resistance

Around October of '68
a CIA Chaos/Project Resistance analyst
whacked out a memo which noted
        "the apparent freedom and ease in which filth,
        slanderous and libelous statements,
        and what appear to be almost treasonous
                anti-establishment propaganda
                        is allowed to circulate"
                                in underground papers.

    The CIA smut-sleuth then suggested a strategy for silencing the underground.

    "Eight out of ten," he wrote, "would fail if a few phonograph record companies stopped advertising in them."

The CIA of course denies it directly carried out the concept of
interdicting the record company moolah stream.

Instead, the FBI did it. In January of '69 the San Francisco office
of the FBI wrote to headquarters
            that Columbia Records
                    by advertising in the underground
            "appears to be giving active aid and comfort to enemies
                            of the United States."

The memo from SF suggested the FBI persuade Columbia Records
            to stop advertising in the underground press

                        It worked
                        By the end of the next year
                many record company ads had been pulled
                & a number of underground papers had folded•

Humphrey went down
            by seven-tenths of a percentage point
                and Nixon was elected

There was a certain amount of frail analysis
among my companions
who felt that the advent of Tricky
                    was the prolegomenon
                            to the victory of the left

Others, such as Allen Ginsberg,
blamed the Yippies and
                the disaster of Chicago
                        for Tricky's advent.

No doubt the kids in the teargas
                were easy to hate
                        by the workaday millions—
lazy and crazy
        as if they had *Bartleby the Scrivener*
                        tattooed across their pot-toking lips

but they were only a few

and cannot be blamed for this:
                Humphrey defeated Humphrey
                    (with a little help from his friends
                                    in Chaos and Garden Plot)

GOVERNMENT

I was always very suspicious
                of the words
                        "The form of government
                                    will grow out of the revolution"

                        Yet part of me
                        always agreed
                        with Proudhon
                        that Property is Theft.

I had this notion
                of a Universal Rent Strike
and in late '68
codified it with "The Universal Rent Strike Rag"
                        (later on my album, *Beer Cans on the Moon*)

I listened to it for the first time
in 25 years
                researching this book
                            and, while not poetry,
                            pays good honor to Proudhon's
                            La propriété, c'est le vol. •

I told Jerry Rubin
            that the Yippies
                ought to form a Shadow Cabinet
                                    that shadowy fall

        and issue decrees
        and prepare themselves to govern

        if they really wanted to forge

a socialist revolution

but in the back of my mind
I wondered if I really wanted
Jerry Rubin or Abbie
the Weathermen
    Eldridge Cleaver
        or even my hero Allen Ginsberg
                running the nation?

No set of mammals in '68
yet had the strength,
        the time, the grit
the genius, the vision
to open the door of America
        to the structure of sharing.

        It had taken almost a decade
        for me to realize
        that I was a democratic socialist
           or a Danish-style Social Democrat

In the years just before World War I
there were 70 socialist mayors in 24 states
1,200 socialist office holders in 340 cities
        And the socialist Meyer London was in the
        House of Representatives
        representing the very
        apartment
           where Miriam, Didi and I
           were living!

Eugene Debs in '12 got 6% of the vote for prez
My mentor Allen Ginsberg
    had once sought to become a labor lawyer
and there were even a few good overtly socialist poets,
           including Carl Sandburg

Meanwhile I tried to confuse my
        sorrow with projects
through the fall of 1968.

I helped create a television film for the Yippies
for which Country Joe McDonald, Ken Pine and I wrote a song
                              called "Chicago"

and I put up the money to publish
a quarterly called the *Marijuana Review*

I collected photographs
for a possible book on Chicago
            but gave it up
            and began notes instead
                        for a satire
                        that I finished
                              in 1969
                              published by Grove Press

    I'd put the Fugs mailing address
                        on our Warner Brothers records
    and the mail poured into Stuyvesant Station
                              by the several thousand
    so I spent several weeks sending newsletters
                        to those who had written

    Hundreds of these letters reside in my Woodstock file cabs
    and I've noticed how many were adorned
    with psychedelic festoonage, eyeballs, peace signs
                              and trembling capitals
    One even contained an LSD-spritzed Necco wafer

    I've often thought of looking up
    30 years later
                some of these people—

damozels willing to take baths in jello
or young guys
                    so determined to be Something Else—
                              to see how they've fared.

I began gathering original art
                    from some underground comic artists
                              whose work I admired
for a show at Peace Eye which opened
                              November 7
I think it was the first
                    underground comic art show
The walls were packed with great works—
pages from R. Crumb's notebooks,
and original strips by Crumb, Art Spiegelman, Kim Deitch,
Bill Beckman and Spain Rodriguez
                    (who drew the invitation)

I sent out a press release
                    with text such as:
"These comic strip plexi are high energy spew-grids
which at their best discharge intense power & beauty
in to the brain as the eye slurps across their surface.
The jolt of such immediate energy creates in the beholder
profound sensations of mirth, anarchy, poetry, sodomy-froth,

Hideum apparitions and somehow, faith. It's not easy.
These artists live & work together, constantly comparing a milllion
ideas and anecdotes, cackling & chortling over the pushy violence
of the world, annotating with their tense disciplined rapidographs
the terror in the wall...."

Peace Eye was packed that night
and so were the fine-drawn walls

Standing in Peace Eye
with the Comic Art on the Wall

November 15 at Hunter College
was Janis Joplin's final NY performance with
Big Brother
and then they flew west for final
concerts in California

I was feeling a little guilty
for urging Janis all that spring
to go out on her own
(though many others also urged)

November 16
Nor Nix nor dread
prevented the celebration of Miriam's birthday

as that day I went to Seashells Unlimited
at 39th and 3rd

and bought some gifts:
a pearled nautilus and an elephant's tusk

from the Philippines
a black abalone and a sea urchin
from off California
a mushroom coral from the Red Sea
a sand dollar from Florida
and a tree snail from Haiti.

Though the phrases "Trance of Sorrow"
and "Universal Joke"
showed up in my notebooks
by the end of the year
I'd never experienced the mood swings
and depressions
befalling a few of my friends

Phil Ochs in particular
began to experience
a late-century version of Fitzgerald's "Crack-Up"

He pulled together some tunes
in the fall and booked time to record
Rehearsals for Retirement.

It had a horrifying cover
a photo of a tombstone
"Phil Ochs (American)
Born: El Paso, Texas 1940
Died: Chicago, Illinois 1968"

I loved to hear him sing
& wished I'd been in Vancouver
for a concert late in the year
Phil sang his setting of Poe's "Bells"
with Allen Ginsberg
on hand to play the
tintinnabulations
on the bells.

The phone always rang.
Abbie told me he had conditioned himself
to be fully awake and ready to discuss anything
the moment he picked up the phone
at 4 AM.

I was impressed
        how in one weekend after Chicago
He'd slaved around the clock
            to finish his book called
                    Revolution for the Hell of It

I thought the title
            told a great deal
                about his psyche
        but I was under the sway of his brilliance
so I worked with Dial Press
and threw a publication party November 22
        the anniversary of JFK
                at the Peace Eye Bookstore

            He signed a copy for me
            on a book plate
            tree whose roots
                    clutched a book:
        "To Ed Sanders
        There are
         but few that get
         to fuck the world
                Abbie"

(There was another Abbie signature
        from around that time
            that helped set his legend—
Movie rights to *Revolution for the Hell of It* were bought by MGM
with an initial payment of $25,000
            Abbie signed the check
            and gave it to the
                Black Panther bail fund)

    During Abbie's party at Peace Eye
    I went down the street
                to get more wine
    There'd been a stick-up
                and a shooting at the liquor store

    It was one of those "400 Blows" moments
    a frozen image of
    an elevated heap of burbly blood on the pavement
    which I stepped over
                to get into the store
                    to buy some Bacchus

November 22 was also the day the
    Beatles White Double Album was released.

    In Death Valley
        in a lonely old dry upper desert ranch
            the Manson group
                listened to the White Double
                    by a gasoline-generator

    and began to believe
    the words of black-white war
                were hidden in the vinyl grooves

            Events were beginning
            to acquire a kind of equality—
    Liverpool & Armageddon—
    jacking off became the same
                    as offing Jack

and I was thirteen months away
from starting to study
                    this strange group of
                              edgy wanderers.

THE BOOK BOAT

Out in California
a young man named John Martin
                    and his wife Barbara
began Black Sparrow Press in '66

By '68 it was one of the finest,
publishing Zukofsky's *A Fragment for Careenagers*,
A Tree Telling of Orpheus by Denise Levertov
Creeley's *The Finger*, and *Greed, Parts I & II* by
Diane Wakoski, *At Terror Street & Agony Way*
by Charles Bukowski, Robert Kelly's *Finding the Measure*,
                    plus tomes by Paul Bowles,
                    McClure, Duncan, Rothenberg,
                    Owens, Dorn, Eshleman & others

They had a belief in books
and I know for sure
that as a kid
books had literally saved my life

Lawrence said to build a Boat of Death
but I was steeped in things Egyptian too
and built a Boat of Books
                    which brought me out of the chaos

Ever since I'd felt I had a Book Boat
a gathering of precious tomes
                    to take me through the rapids

But now, at the end of a teargas year
(even though I owned a book store
          with almost instant access to any I wanted}
I lost their succour

Books were
	falling from the
sides of my boat
		and water was rushing in.

I wasn't sure what to do
I thought maybe I'd copy Ferlinghetti
			and begin a serious publishing house
give up music
pretend Avenue A was the Euphrates
and build a cabin of books again
			as if they were mud and wattles

and then on November 24
a dreadful telephone call
my friend d.a. levy
		shot himself
			in the third eye
sitting lotus
	on a mattress
		in a nearly empty pad
				in Cleveland

using his childhood .22
	and triggering the shot
			with his toe

Since we'd talked in August
he'd begun to give away his things
broke up with his wife

In the fall he'd gone to Madison
to be the poet in residence
			at the Free University

He taught a course in telepathy
	which he did not attend
though the class met anyway
	and focussed on levy from afar

He made some brilliant collages in Madison

and then in November he returned
                              to Cleveland

He wrote a final lengthy poem,
                with its haunting lines
                "i don't know
                poetry seemed like such
                a good idea
                a way to communicate
                pretty pictures
                or to see things that exist
                now. But the people want blood."

I heard he was moving to the Coast
I think he hated to be driven from Cleveland
but the poverty that haunted Hart Crane
                              smashed him without mercy

The issues of
                economic justice
                              and personal freedom
which wore out the good bard levy

have not yet
                been addressed
                              in America
so that a shyer & less-pushy genius
                              can flourish a proper span

1968 was the year
Lord Byron finally got his plaque
in the Poets Corner
                at Westminister Abbey

It sometimes takes centuries
                to sort out a poet
                              and so it may be for
                                   darryl allan levy
                                        of Cleveland

November 27
    Eldridge Cleaver fled to Europe
    on the day he was to surrender for parole violation
        The CIA followed him
                as a fascinating threat
                      to national security

The Fugs November 29–30
    Played the Kaleidoscope Theater
        at 4445 Main Street in Philadelphia
        for $2700 bucks

The place was outfitted
    with hundreds of sofas
        upon which the audience
      toked and erotically disported
           during our gig

December 15
    Ted Berrigan wrote me from Iowa City
          where he was teaching poetry at the University:

"Dear Ed,
    thanks for the poem, and the records, and papers. The
    new album is inspirational. Sandy likes Crystal Liaison
 best, not knowing it's RC.... and I
    like all of it, especially Ramses II is daid and
      the last cut on side one whose name I don't recall.
      There's a real feeling for quietness, sepulchralness
 (is that a word) and death throughout. A kind of awful
  hush filled with song that's fitting and so saying the
critic took another pull on his stogie and then nodded
      out

    Levy's suicide was a kick in the gut. A terrible
  disappointment, tho not in him of course... what's it
all about....
    is what it released in my heart awfully....
If you do his book, you might try to get some of his collages
  The few I've seen were quite nice and
    and quite beautiful in some ways..."

December 16
    the Spanish government
        finally got around to voiding
           the 1492 decree expelling Jews from Spain

    It was the same day that Valerie Solanas
        got out of Mattewan State Hospital
    and the judge declared her competent to stand trial
                    for shooting Andy

December 19–22
    the Fugs were in New Haven
        for gigs at the Stone Balloon
    We were very, very weary
    though the band was tighter than ever
    sharp & bitter & full of ferality
    though nothing could overcome
        the décadance
           that was chewing our work
    like mice in a box of archives.

THE OSTRACIZED ELF

Another career I was thinking of pursuing
was as a producer for Warner Brothers/Reprise
I could book studio time at will
    and Reprise would pay for it
They'd sent me a private book with other Warner producers & acts
        (It even had Sinatra's number)
so I wrote a Christmas story called "The Ostracized Elf"
which I printed as a New Year's card
    to send to my associates in the biz

It was a variation on the Rudolph fable:

Osbert, the story went, was a long haired hippie elf
whose specialty in the North Pole toy factory
    was Shell Stations with adjoining hippie communes

240

When Santa ordered Osbert not to make any more pipes
and weird toys, Osbert dared to argue, and Santa tossed him out.

Osbert, the tale continued,
stood outside the toy factory and wept.

For days he stood there in the snow
watching the frenzy of packing and singing elves.
Everybody noticed Osbert's nose
            steaming the glass but pretended not to see him.
Santa was heading out on Christmas Eve
Osbert the ostracized turned his wet face to Santa
and said the miracle words, "Merry Christmas, Santa."
Santa himself began to weep
            in a moment revealing what I longed for—
            the spiritual power of reconcilation,
"Osbert how would you like to ride with me tonight
                        in the front seat of the sleigh?"
after which Kringle and Osbert the elf flew above the habitation,
shouting and singing in pre-K-Mart jubilation
                        no doubt planting a few
                  unusual Shell Stations
                     on Avenues B and C.

On Christmas eve
the phone rang
        Andy answered
            to his horror it was Valerie

She was free on bail
and wanted all criminal charges dropped
some roles in upcoming films
and Andy to purchase her manuscripts for $20K
                  plus help her get some
                        guest shots on TV shows

        (not long later, February 25, 1969
            she pled guilty
            and on June 9, '69 was sentenced to three years)

241

Also on Christmas eve
      3 astronauts on Apollo 8
            were the first to orbit the moon
                  Ten times they whirled the circuit
           with a live telecast we savored
        and then they wended home

          I was beginning to worry about
          this journey into outer space
          that it was not such
             a Santa Claus benevolence trip

          that we were crossing
                 the great Iron Void
         like Hesiod's
            anvil into tartaros
        or, maybe worse,
                like the hostile spores of metastasis.

It all seemed quite benevolent, however,
watching the moon on Avenue A
      with Miriam stringing tinsel
           in neat patterns on a tree
and Deirdre excited about Santa,
hanging stockings
       on our marble fireplace

There was a Christmas reading at the St. Mark's Church
          for the Poetry Project—
    a huge list of names, myself, Joe Brainard,
    Anne Waldman, Peter Schjeldahl, Kenward Elmslie
             and oodles of bardic Other

The day after Christmas
the Fugs flew to Cleveland,
      for a three day gig at Le Cave

242

I tried to learn what I could about d. a. levy's
suicide

Some bikers came back stage at Le Cave
              and spiked our drinks
                        maybe with STP

Whatever it was
          it was another one of those Ultimate Spinach trips
          which I had to carry out in a Howard Johnson motel
          I called Miriam
                    to have her talk me down from the spinach
                              (as she had in '66
                                        when I called during a
                                        psilocybin trip with Olson and Weaver
                                                            in Gloucester)

          Things didn't turn out as well for our bass player
          who was almost paralyzed the next day
          when we had to take the train to Chicago
                              because a snowstorm had closed the airport

At the Chicago gig
        we told him just to hold his bass
                        and not to try to play

(A few days later
        he was grabbed at JFK
                trying to get back to London
                        convinced he was Paul McCartney!

He had a beautiful voice
and he soon returned from the Visionary Other
                and stayed with us for the
                        remaining months of the 1960s Fugs)

Our gig in Chicago was at the Aragon Ballroom.
                        with Wilson Pickett!
We couldn't wait to hear him sing his hits,
                "In the Midnight Hour" & "Mustang Sally"
Unfortunately, Pickett was kept by the snow
                        from coming to Chicago

and the Fugs,
        one of our players in a stupor
faced a rather surly audience
                who were told the lead act wasn't there
                and they weren't getting their money back

It was in this context,
        that when I called Mayor Richard Daley a motherfucker
        the restless crowd of 5,000
                        didn't take it well
        A woman directly in front of me
                        tossed a container of coca cola
                        in my face
                & we fled to our hotel
                the fancy Astor Towers
                        to party

Next we hopped up to Detroit
to play the Grande Ballroom
                December 30

and the next day flew to LaGuardia
                              and back to 196 Avenue A

On New Year's eve
Miriam and I got dressed up
and went down the street
to Pee Wee's bar and restaurant

Pee Wee was a wide-faced one-eyed guy
who ran a friendly multiracial place

At midnight we clinked our
champagne glasses together
                    and leaned across the table
                    as we did every year, for a good luck kiss
            and said goodbye to 1968

just as now
            on a computer screen
a hundred miles away
                    from where we kissed
I say farewell again o '68
May you rest in your
                              inky vestiges!

Reside! o '68
            in the books and boxes
                        of my writing studio
                    so many years from
                    Grant Park, My Lai, Memphis
                                & Kennedy clutching
                                        his rosary

Pee Wee's was packed
when we clinked together our
                        champagne glasses
                in the *dum spiro spero*
                mode of our thirsty generation.

We whistled, we shouted
            we stamped on the sawdust floor

while in my soul
        a year-long carillon of bells was tolling

They were tolling
            for the shrapneled dead in the jungles
            the leafless forests, the napalm and mines
They were tolling for Kennedy's
            small white cross in Arlington
They were tolling for the centuries it takes
            to make a country more benign
For the bells of d.a. levy's Cherokee Ponies
The bells of Poe in Baltimore
                    that Phil Ochs sang
                            and Allen rang

For the bells on the tear gas grenades
            Allen and I sprinted through
                to get back to the Hotel Lincoln
The sweet sound
        of Didi's wrist bell
                    on Avenue A
The bells of the St. Nicholas Carpatho-Russian church
            two hundred feet from the Peace Eye Bookstore
The bells the bells
            sounding in a new year
                    on the Avenue

All your inky fury is gone, o year—
but the struggle
        for freedom
            & a just, sharing world
            where no one is hungry or cold
                is always in the air

No police state
        Cointelpro or Chaos
    no teargas truck no battle-maddened mind
            no urge to control & enslave
                can stop that struggle
                    or erase it.

Farewell, o '68

p. 10   Indicted for conspiring to counsel young men to evade the draft were Dr. Benjamin Spock, author of the ultrapopular *Baby and Child Care*, the Rev. William Sloane Coffin chaplain of Yale University, Harvard grad student Michael Ferber, novelist Mitchell Goodwin, and Marcus Raskin of the Institute for Policy Studies

        In a trial later in the year
        Raskin was acquitted
        the others were found guilty
                and sentenced to 2 years

        As Kirkpatrick Sales noted in his book *SDS*, page 406, it was "the first unmistakable signal that the left faced a serious threat of repression."

p. 10   Not long after the October '67 Exorcism and March
        on the Pentagon
        Attorney General Ramsey Clark
        ordered the creation of "Interdivision Information Unit"
        known as IDIU, in Justice Dept, to collect data
                on Vietnam war & leftist dissent
        IDIU got info from Army Intelligence, from
        FBI, and other "Federal organizations."

p. 12   The Fugs had signed a multi-album contract with Atlantic Records in early '67. We worked hard on our first album for Atlantic, recording it at Talentmaster studio on 42nd Street. We completed it, and the response from a group of Atlantic executives for whom we played it was good. Then I received a terse phonecall announcing that we were tossed off the label. Our managers heard some scuttlebutt from Albert Grossman that the reason we were tossed from Atlantic was that, since Atlantic was negotiating to sell to Warner Brothers, they didn't want the Fugs lowering their sale price. If that were true, then it's ironic that we soon were given a contract by Warner/Reprise for whom we recorded four albums in the late 1960s.

        Meanwhile, we had a lost a crucial year, 1967, during which we did not release any albums. In early '68, our album *Tenderness Junction* came out, which was comprised of elements of our banished Atlantic album, plus new songs we had added, such as a version of the Fugs/Diggers "Exorcism of the Pentagon."

p. 17 The Avalon Ballroom was at Sutter and Van Ness
The concert was produced by Chet Helm's Family Dog Productions.

p. 22 Sirhan had been raised as a Christian Arab
in Old City, Jerusalem
One of five sons belonging to Mary and Bishara Sirhan
In Jan, '57 came to U.S. with mother and dad,
two brothers and sister
By mid '57 dad had deserted them and gone back to Palestine
Sirhan attended John Muir High in Pasadena,
and went to Pasadena City College couple of years
then wanted to become a jockey

He was an exercise boy at Granja Vista Del Rio Horse Ranch in Corona, east of L.A.

Sept. '66 tossed from galloping horse
Applied for workman's comp

Then worked for health food store in Pasadena
as stock boy and driver
Got settlement, $1,705, and quit health food store
according to the book *R.F.K. Must Die*, by Robert B. Kaiser

The Question of Robowash.
I think that the prevailing mood in the media is that the facts of programmed assassin research should not be spread among civilians because of strong certainty that cults, terrorists, and militias, not to mention governments big and small, would put the techniques to use.

Nevertheless, it seems certain also that the U.S. military-intelligence apparatus, well prior to the assassinations of Martin Luther King and Robert Kennedy, had developed techniques to alter memory, implant false memories, erase memories and create programmed couriers, agents with no recall, and programmed killers.

It's a scary subject, not only that the techniques likely already were used to alter the history, say, of 1968, but that the techniques are ready to be used now, three decades after the slayings of '68, in an age where more and more control is being placed upon populations, more and more surveillance, and more and more of what is known as "psy-war" is used for the swaying of nations.

There is no space here for a full explication of U.S. military/ CIA research into mind control. In 1962, after President Kennedy tried to shake up the CIA following the Bay of Pigs, the CIA had already been studying mind control for ten years. The mind program was called MKULTRA till June 1964, when it became MKSearch. MKSearch went on throughout the 1960s and early '70s, under the CIA's Office of Research and Development (ORD).

Richard Helms became director of the CIA in 1967. He was a "protector of unfettered behavorial research," wrote John Marks in his very informative book, *The Search for the "Manchurian Candidate"—The CIA and Mind Control—The Secret History of the Behavorial Sciences.* (Dell Publishing, 1988). During those years, the CIA's Office of Research and Development (ORD) worked steadily on robotic control techniques. Creating amnesia was a priority. There was research into techniques of brain surgery using electrode probes in order to sever "past memory and present recall," to use Mr. Marks' words (page 225). The CIA seems to have developed a drug that helps program new memories into the mind of an amnesiac subject.

Another interesting book, in which the CIA was accused of programming an alternate personality into a courier, is *The Control of Candy Jones*, by Donald Bain (Playboy Press, 1976). For a few years during the 1970s I worked on a book about the Robert Kennedy assassination, and learned that the man Candy Jones said was her CIA control was a doctor who lived on Lexington Drive in Beverly Hills. I once took photographs of the communications aerial on his roof, to see if it might be operating on government frequencies.

John Marks wrote *The Search for the "Manchurian Candidate"* based on about seven boxes of CIA documents from the 1950s obtained by him under the Freedom of Information Act, plus numerous interviews. In early 1973 Richard Nixon fired CIA director Richard Helms. Helms oversaw a huge destruction of documents and tapes, including the files on mind control. Seven boxes were burned, but they forgot to burn another seven boxes of financial records relating to MKULTRA mind control research, and another three boxes belonging to a mind-bend project called ARTICHOKE. These ten boxes from the 1950s MKULTRA research became the basis for Marks' book.

In the meantime, while he was writing his book, Marks heard of mind research that was done in the 1960s and early 1970s by the CIA's Office of Research and Development. (ORD had a rural center out of Boston in which it did much of its research) Marks filed under FOIA for CIA files of mind research done by ORD, and was told in reply that there were 130 boxes of relevant material. As far as I know, no one, including Mr. Marks, has ever looked at any of these 130 boxes of 1960s robo-wash files. Perhaps some young sleuths should go after these boxes.

Another book with interesting information on robowash is *Operation Mind Control—Our Secret Government's War Against Its Own People*, by Walter Bowart (Dell Publishing 1978). Other books with pertinent information are *The Assassination of Robert F. Kennedy*, by John Christian and William Turner (Random House, 1978), and *"R.F.K. Must Die!" A History of the Robert Kennedy Assassination and its Aftermath* by Robert Blair Kaiser (E.P. Dutton 1970).

p. 26   It was published that we had peed on Joseph's McCarthy's grave, which is not true, just as we had NOT done the same to the walls of the Pentagon during the '67 Exorcism. In its own unique way, this ceremony was serious.

p. 32   CIA Operation Chaos. Though much of Operation Chaos is still stupidly kept secret, some fragments have emerged over the years, such as Seymour Hersh's exposés in early 1975 in *The New York Times*. For instance, in late 1967 an Army military intelligence agent named Ralph Stein (later an attorney) gave a secret briefing to some CIA officers on domestic dissent.

The briefing was arranged by the CIA liaison to Army counterintelligence offices.

There were three or four elderly gents
                    from the Agency

They seemed very familiar
        with subjects
                such as SDS publications
        and the *Berkeley Barb*

and asked a lot of questions

Ralph Stein was a military counterintelligence
agent from '65 to '68
                    (see *New York Times*, January 11, 1975)

The CIA's Domestic Surv
        in the '60s
        was done under the aegis of
        James Angleton's Counterintelligence section

In a memo of August 15, 1967 then head of covert ops
Thomas Karamessines suggested
that Harry Rositzke and Richard Ober
            head what became known as CHAOS
                    (*Denver Post* July 9, 1975)

        Richard Ober was the Chaos liaison with Richard Helms
                    (head of the CIA in '68)
        Had regular and unique direct access to Helms

        Ober assembled a large staff
        and acquired huge amounts of data

According to the Rockefeller Commission
    Chaos indexed 300,000 names, kept 13,000 subject files,
    and collected huge numbers of intercepted letters
    and cables from the subjects

                William Colby
                testified in January of '75
                that the CIA had placed
                (or recruited)
                at least 22 CIA agents
    in "American dissident circles"

and that Richard Helms on August 15, 1967
authorized CIA counterintelligence division
to look into foreigners
            linked with American radicals
                    (*NY Times* Jan 16, 1975)

        In mid-1969 Special Operations Group (Chaos)
            had 36 positions which increased by 18
        in the spring of '71.
                    (*Denver Post* July 9, 1975)

Let's let Alexander Pope end this note on Chaos,
with the final quatrain from the *Dunciad*:

Lo! thy dread empire, Chaos! is restored;
Light dies before thy uncreating word;
Thy hand, great Anarch! lets the curtain fall,
And universal darkness buries all.

p. 33   Information on Project Resistance was pulled out of the gov-
ernment by the Center for National Security Studies.

p. 33   Here's the fullest version I could find of Hoover's famous
March 4, 1968 proclamation updating the "Black Nationalists"
program:

"For maximum effectiveness of the Counterintelligence Program,
and to prevent wasted effort, long-range goals are being set.

1. Prevent the coalition of militant black nationalist groups. In
unity there is strength; a truism that is not less valid for all its triteness.
An effective coalition of black nationalist groups might be the first step
toward a real 'Mau Mau' in America, the beginning of a true black
revolution.

2. Prevent the rise of a 'Messiah' who could unify, and electrify the
militant black nationalist movement. ████████ might have been such a
'messiah'; he is the martyr of the movement today. ████████ all aspire
to this position. ████████ is less of a threat because of his age.
████████ is a very real contender for this position should he abandon
his supposed 'obedience' to 'white, liberal doctrines'—nonviolence—and
embrace black nationalism. ████████ has the necessary charisma to
be a real threat in this way.

3. Prevent violence on the part of black nationalist groups...
Through counter-intelligence it should be possible to pinpoint potential
troublemakers and neutralize them before they exercise their potential for
violence.

4. Prevent militant black nationalist groups and leaders from
gaining *respectibility* by discrediting them to three separate segments of
the community...the responsible Negro community;...the responsible
(white) community and to 'liberals;'...(and) in the eyes of Negro radi-
cals, the followers of the movement...

5. A final goal should be to prevent the long-range *growth* of
militant black nationalist organization, especially among youth. Specific
tactic to prevent these groups from converting young people must be
developed."

p. 35   On Codrescu's bust. I asked him about it, and he replied, "I
was arrested for pot and guns!"

p. 38   To get the scope of early Yippie, you can look at the various committees that Hoffman had set up, as on this letterhead:

Festival of Life

MUSIC
Jerry Brandt
Judy Collins
Al Cooper
Bob Fass
Michael Goldstein
Richard Goldstein
Bill Graham
Harold Leventhal
Joe MacDonald
Michael Ochs
Ellen Sender
Ed Sanders
Jack Solomon
Andy Wickham

THEATRE
Eric Bentley
Ed Bullins
Jim Fourett
Saul Gottlieb
Allen Kaprow
Jacques Levy
Robert Macbeth
John O/Neal
Richard Schechner
Peter Schumann
Enrique Vargas
Douglas Turner Ward

ART
Diane di Prima
Gary Grimshore
George Herms
Tiger Morse
Carol Sheber
Gerd Stern
Jud Yalkut

NEWSPAPER
Ed Beardsley
Marshall Bloom
John Bryant
Allen Cohen
Marvin Garson
Martin Jezer
Alan Katzman
Ray Mungo
Collin Pearson
Max Xcheer

RELIGION
Allen Ginsberg
Paul Krassner
Timothy Leary

FILM
Joe Cohen
Marvin Fishman
Norm Fruchter
Peter Gessner

SEX
Tuli Kupferberg
Alan Marlowe

GAMES
Abbie Hoffman
Keith Lampe
Abe Peckolick
Hugh Romney
Jerry Rubin
Gloria Yippie

YOUTH INTERNATIONAL PARTY † 32 Union Square East † New York, N.Y. 10003 † (212) 982-5090

Milton Glazer donated a poster to sell as did the 2nd Avenue music commune Group Image. There was enough money to open a YIP office at room 607, 32 Union Square East.

There were a number of activists who contributed time and talent to early Yippie. These include Jeff Shero, Brad Fox, Super Joel, Sam and Walli Leff, Bob Fass, Paul Krassner, Stew Albert, Wolf Lowenthal, Abe Peck, Kate Coleman, Marty and Susan Carey, Paul McIsaac, Robin Palmer, and numerous others.

p. 45   The Gold Crisis of '68
a murky thing
   difficult to fathom

It may have had to
do with France
            hoarding gold
to punish the U.S.
            for Vietnam
(They were apparently upset with France
for having oodles of gold
while at the same time
            spending oodles for labor peace)
The Chinese also were under suspicion
            for aurum-hoarding
Anyway, there had been a multiyear run
on U.S. gold reserves
and the U.S. and allies began to set aside
            the gold standard
(As for the European countries
making peace with their labor unions,
it may take the U.S. another century
to learn that Social Democracy
is the price Capital pays
            for peace in the streets)

p. 46   ee ee ee ee
         this comes from the final lines of Euripides' *Trojan Women*,
         with the chorus singing an *ee* as sacked Troy burns and
         women and children are being loaded in the boats as booty.

p. 46   Minneapolis Honeywell manufactured fragmentation bombs.

p. 62   Here's the innocent looking Yip-in poster:

sometimes with the goal of "pure harassment."
O'Brien's Mil-Int reports
were passed to FBI, Secret Service, Chicago PD, et al.

The 113th Military Intelligence Group
received 3 or 4 cartons of doc's stolen
from the Chicago Seven defense office
by the right wing Legion of Justice
a group which was being financially supported
by Mil-Int, as reported
by Sanford Ungar in the *Washington Post*
November 14, 1973

The Legion of Justice
threw gas bombs and disrupted
perf's of Russian Moiseyev Dance Company
and Chinese acrobats
in '70 & '72

One of the grenades was traced to "army stocks"
the *New York Post* reported, May 1, 1975

p. 125   Peter Noyes. See his book, *Legacy of Doubt.* Noyes was a news editor at KABC television in L.A.

p. 126   Peter Edmiston and Charles Rothschild were the managers of the Fugs, and, against many odds, kept us successfully on the road throughout the late 1960s.

p. 126   The San Francisco Mime Troupe had been busted for obscenity during free performances in the parks.

p. 126   Fugs at the Fillmore. The additional musicians were Richard Tee, Carl Lynch, Howard Johnson, and Julius Watkins, with the ensemble conducted by Warren Smith. In addition we added a harmony singer. We rented recording equipment from Hanley Sound, and Richard Alderson recorded the concerts.

p. 131   Soviet tanks and troops
Soviets feared that Czechoslovakia would leave
Warsaw pact and declare itself neutral,
thus breaching the buffer zone across Eastern Europe
in place since WW II

257

announced it wanted to bring 100,000
    McCarthy supporters
        to Chicago
           to open up the Convention

but Daley denied the Coalition a permit to
           march on the convention hall

Lowenstein went to court
but on August 22
Judge William Lynch, Daley's former law partner,
           denied the appeal

p. 183   "Jim Morrison." For years I wasn't sure of his real name. Now, I know, and he's a very respected environmentalist and educator, and, heh heh, saying no to temptation, pass over his name.

p. 184   MC5—Rob Tyner, Wayne Kramer, Fred Smith, Michael Davis, and Dennis Thompson

p. 195   Burroughs, Ginsberg, Genet and Southern had press
passes to get into the convention.
When I asked him what was going
        on on the inside of the convention
Burroughs chuckle-laughed
        in his growlly St. Louis blues voice
and played me a crackly, whirry tape
he said he'd played from the balcony
        of the convention hall
If I understood him correctly
it was a Confusion Tape
deliberately designed to spread chaos

It worked, Bill, it worked.

p. 201   On McCarthy refusing to carry his bid to the convention floor. He was a reserved guy, and not a high metabolism quester. Perhaps he felt that Humphrey had a "secret plan" to end the war. After all, Nixon claimed to have one later on that fall. Behind the hesitance, I think, was a fear of the military, as in Charles Olson's line, "Blood is the food of those gone mad."

p. 209   New Penelope at 378 Sherbrooke St. West
        owned by a guy named Gary Eisenkraft

p. 211   Here's a page from my FBI files, dated October 10, 1968:

```
UNI   D STATES DEPARTMENT OF J  TICE
        FEDERAL BUREAU OF INVESTIGATION


Date      October 10, 1968              Office  CHICAGO


Title     ED SANDERS


Synopsis  ED SANDERS, a leader of the Youth International Party
          (Yippies) and leader of the rock music group "The Fugs,"
          was in Chicago, Illinois, in connection with the
          Democratic National Convention (DNC) during August 26-
          30, 1968.
                                           he was not
          involved in demonstrations or activities. AUSA, Chicago
          on 10/7/68, declined prosecution.
```

p. 214   The same day, October 1,
        in Mexico City
            hemic bash-clash
                students and police
      toward the end of nine-week student strike
      The government desperate to get the country
      quiet for the Olympics just a few days away

p. 220   See EXTENT OF SUBVERSION IN CAMPUS DISORDERS
*Hearings before the Subcommittee to Investigate the Admini-
stration of the Internal Security Act and Other Internal
Security Laws of the Committee on the Judiciary* United
States Senate   June 26 1969   U.S. Government Printing
Office   Washington 1969

p. 227   See "Sabotaging the Dissident Press" pp. 164–165 by Angus
Mackenzie, in *Unamerican Activities*, in the Pen American
Center Report, *The Campaign Against the Underground
Press*, by Geoffrey Rips; edited by Anne Janowitz and Nancy
J. Peters; City Lights Books, 1981

p. 228   *The Universal Rent Strike Rag*

When the last grim government is gone, my friend
And the last landlord is through

And the last policeman has thrown away his gun
And the last wire tap is done

And the Legions of Green are walking along
                    with their plastic shillelaghs held high
And the last computer has computed its last
                    and the Flags of Fantasy fly!

Oh birth, death, sex, gossip, politics, religion
Oh sing that Universal Rent Strike Rag
Not going to be anything left to do
        but that Universal Rent Strike Rag!

When the plastic plexidomes are built on the moon
Socialist algae tanks are turning out cream
We'll sit by the banks of the hydroponic stream
And cackle and chortle in the Universal Dream

The last police state falls on the floor
Clothes are free at the dry goods store
The last hungry stomach is feasted full
The only thing left to talk about more

Birth, death, sex, gossip, politics, religion
Sing that Universal Rent Strike Rag
There's not going to be anything left to do
But that Universal Rent Strike Rag....

Printed May 1997 in Santa Barbara
& Ann Arbor for the Black Sparrow Press by
Mackintosh Typography & Edwards Brothers Inc.
Text set in Korinna by Words Worth.
Design by Barbara Martin.
This first edition is published in paper wrappers;
there are 200 hardcover trade copies;
100 hardcover copies have been numbered &
signed by the author; & 20 copies lettered
A–T have been handbound in boards by
Earle Gray & signed by the author.

PHOTO: Dion Ogust

*Edward Sanders wearing
the pulse lyre gloves*

EDWARD SANDERS lives in Woodstock, N.Y. with his wife of over 36 years, the writer and painter Miriam R. Sanders. Together they publish a newspaper, the *Woodstock Journal.*

Sanders graduated from New York University in 1964, with a degree in Classics. His recent CD, *Songs in Ancient Greek,* features his settings of Homer, Sappho, Archilochus, Simonides, Aristophanes, Plato and Ecclesiastes. His 1993 musical drama, *Cassandra,* is based on texts from Euripides, Homer, Aeschylus, and Apollodorus, with sections chanted and sung in Greek meters.

In 1965 he founded the Fugs, a folk rock satire group which has, during its thirty-two year history, issued a wide assortment of albums and CDs. Among Fugs CDs currently available are *The Real Woodstock Festival* (a two-CD set, 1995) and *Songs from a Portable Forest* (the best of the Fugs revival shows from the 1980s), and early albums such as *The Fugs First Album* (1965) and *The Fugs* (second album, 1966), and the 1984 classic, *Refuse to Be Burnt Out.*

Sanders' 1971 book, *The Family,* the story of the Charles Manson group, remains in print in a number of countries. He has written a three-volume collection of interrelated short stories, *Tales of Beatnik Glory,* and is at work on the fourth and final volume. In the field of musical inventions, he has developed some novel instruments—the Bardic Pulse Lyre, the Talking Tie, the Light Lyre, the Mona Lisa Lyre, and the Microlyre, the latter a microtonal keyboard.

He has received several writing awards, including a Guggenheim Fellowship in poetry and an NEA poetry fellowship. His *Thirsting for Peace in a Raging Century, Selected Poems 1961–1985,* won an American Book Award in 1988.

Black Sparrow Press has published two other books by Sanders—*Hymn to the Rebel Cafe,* and *Chekhov, A Biography in Verse.* It was the good time the author had in writing *Chekhov* that inspired him to undertake *1968, A History in Verse.*